# Raja Yoga

# Raja Yoga

## A Path to Super Conscious Bliss

*A Christian Yogi's Commentary on the Yoga Darsan of Patanjali, His Sutras*

**Sri Joseph Ketron**
**Master of Yoga Education**

Writers Club Press
New York  Lincoln  Shanghai

**Raja Yoga**
A Path to Super Conscious Bliss

All Rights Reserved © 2003 by Joseph M. Ketron III

No part of this book may be reproduced or transmitted in any form or by any means, graphic, electronic, or mechanical, including photocopying, recording, taping, or by any information storage retrieval system, without the written permission of the publisher.

Writers Club Press
an imprint of iUniverse, Inc.

For information address:
iUniverse, Inc.
2021 Pine Lake Road, Suite 100
Lincoln, NE 68512
www.iuniverse.com

ISBN: 0-595-25854-9

Printed in the United States of America

Dedicated to:

Joe Jo Ketron, Carmen Ketron, Rosie Taylor, Caroline Rogers, Kat Reis, Dr. V. S. Rao, Sri Sankara, Lord Christ and, of course, Maharishi Patanjali and all Saints and Sages and persons of knowledge and spirituality.

# Contents

FOREWORD ................................................................................. ix
INTRODUCTION ........................................................................ xi
PREFACE .................................................................................... xvii
Chapter 1:    SAMADHI PADA—ON CONCENTRATION ............. 1
INTRODUCTION TO CHAPTER TWO ........................................ 31
Chapter 2:    SADHANA PADA—ON PRACTICE ......................... 35
INTRODUCTION TO CHAPTER THREE: VIBHUTI
    PADA—ON ATTAINMENT .................................................... 61
Chapter 3:    VIBHUTI PADA—ON ATTAINMENT ..................... 63
Chapter 4:    KAIVALYA PADA—ON INDEPENDENCE .............. 99
FINAL COMMENTARY ............................................................... 113
AUTHOR BIOGRAPHY ................................................................ 117

# FOREWORD

Around 5,000 years ago, about the time the Mayans of Central America were contemplating the concept of zero—the first civilization to do so—another group of people were settling in Northern India. They were known as the Aryans. It is not certain where the Aryans came from but many historians have suggested Central Asia. The Aryans were some of the first people to start diverting their attention from earthly struggles, and to start contemplating the Mind, its power and its connection to the Universe as a whole.

This was the beginning of Yoga.

Around 200 B.C. a man gathered all the current available data on the subject of Yoga from many of the sages around India and wrote what is now known as the "Yoga Sutras" or "Darsan." His name was Maharishi Patanjali. I will explain in my Preface how the words "Darsan" and "Sutras" have been defined because the definitions can vary from teacher to teacher.

There are 22 million Americans practicing Yoga. They range from Madonna, and Kareem Abdul Jabar, to the members of the New York Giants and suburban housewives. Less than ten percent of these practitioners have read the "Yoga Sutras." Many teachers may tell their students that the Sutras are difficult to read and understand. The difficulty lies in the fact that Hindus were the first to make most of the transliterations of the Sutras from ancient Sanskrit. Likewise their corresponding commentaries were presented from a Hindu's perspective whereas almost 80 percent of American Yoga practitioners have Judeo-Christian backgrounds.

As history tells us, by 1888 Yoga was almost forgotten and was only being practiced by small groups in India. T. Krishnamacharya, the teacher of B.K.S. Iyengar and Indra Devi, two well-known Masters, is credited with bringing Yoga back into the limelight by sequencing poses or postures and assigning to them therapeutic value. When the Yoga revival began in earnest in the 1930's, the people in India were living in the same conditions they were living in two thousand years ago. Most of the students were only interested in the aches and pains they had from certain types of activity (and inactivity) and not the upper-level thought processes that may have contributed to some of those problems. Those processes have to be explained slowly. Just as you would not try to explain quantum physics to the average sixth grader, it is not wise to introduce Yoga by way of its more complex aspects. Although it is my belief that those upper-level thought processes are at the present being explained too slowly by the Yoga community.

When Yoga was introduced to America in the early 1950's, students almost universally embraced the postures as a way to look better, feel better and relax. While these are an important and integral part of Yoga, Yoga is much more than those sensory perceptions. In a recent poll conducted by the Yoga *Journal*, a periodical devoted to Yoga; it was revealed that only 16 percent of the respondents were looking to Yoga as a "path to enlightenment." So it looks like nothing has changed in the last 50 years.

The Yoga Sutras contain some of the most fascinating information to which I have had the privilege of being exposed. The New Testament of the Bible has been discussed for 1,950 years. Although both Ralph Waldo Emerson and Henry David Thoreau were introduced to the Bhagavad-Gita in the early 1800s and its influence shows in their literary works, "The Yoga Sutras of Patanjali" have only been discussed in depth in America since 1950. I hope this book will shed more light upon the Sutras so the discussions will continue and progress.

Sri Joseph Ketron<br>
Degree of Master of Yoga of Education

# INTRODUCTION

When I told a friend of mine that I was getting a Masters Degree in Yoga Science and Education he asked me, "are you going to wear a red dot on your forehead?" I explained to him that placing a red dot on one's forehead is a tradition of the Hindus. Yoga is a Science of the mind, not a religion. (The definition given in Webster's Dictionary for science: noun: a systemized study or knowledge of any one department of the mind or matter. In Yogic Science it is believed that there is an indivisible continuum between body and mind, mind and matter.) Should I decide to put a mark on my forehead to let people know who my Deity is, it will be a cross. However, if I have to put a cross on my forehead, or wear one around my neck for people to recognize me as a Christian, I am probably not doing a very good job of being a Christian or a Yogi. People should be able to recognize me as such from my actions. The actions one makes on the paths to becoming "Christ-like" and mastering Yoga are not identical but they are intertwined. I have mastered neither; I am simply on the path.

The late Reverend Swami Satchidananda wrote "Truth is one, paths are many."

When early settlers explored North America and other lands, their paths were never in straight lines—the shortest distance between two points. In their paths they discovered numerous natural obstacles, such as mountains and rivers. Lord Christ, once told his disciples, "If you had faith the size of a mustard seed, you could move a mountain." His disciples nor the early explorers ever attained that degree of faith. The explorers had to go around or bypass the obstacles. In the third chapter of the "Yoga Sutras," Patanjali explains the actual mechanics of how to move a mountain with your mind. You must first scrutinize what harm it would cause the inhabitants of the mountain. If you do not want to move a mountain with your mind, you might want to see through it. That supernatural power is also explained.

In the fourth chapter of the Yoga Sutras, Patanjali metaphorically describes a Yoga teacher as an agriculturist. A field or garden littered with stones, limbs or other debris would be difficult to irrigate. The agriculturist has to remove the obstacles before the flow of water can run unimpeded from its source. Likewise, a Yoga teacher removes the obstacles from a student's mind so that knowledge and consciousness may flow freely and continuously from its source, the Infinite Supreme Being. According to Patanjali, it is only our minds that hinder and restrain us from achieving absolute oneness with the so-called Infinite Supreme Being.

Although I am a Christian, I acknowledge all religions. There is too much scriptural testimony to deny the existence of the central figures upon which other religions are based. All of these religion's paths to know *Truth* are parallel. When you think of parallels, the first impression that might surface in your mind is that of two lines equidistant apart that never meet. However, if one looks at a globe of the earth, the lines from the two poles are also called parallels. At the equator, the distance between these lines is greater than if you were to follow them in either direction from the equator to the poles where they coalesce at a point.

Imagine that the paths spiritual seekers take to know *Truth* are these parallel lines. What separates these paths at the equator is not mere space but language, dogma, theology, scriptural testimony, myth, central figures and, unfortunately, political hierarchies. Once these differences are removed, they all come together on one central point, the belief in an Infinite Supreme Being or Infinite Universe.

Tai Tsung, second emperor of the Tang Dynasty, said, "You have your truth, another theirs. They are equally false; the only real truth belongs to no one."

The history of everyone's religion needs to be preserved and respected. Kriya Yoga suggests that students with restless non-concentrating minds should study *their* religious scriptures or read something spiritually uplifting every day. There is scientific proof that the worship of God will produce positive results in one's life, such as faith healing (this will be explained in Chapter Three). It is also a historical fact that people who have misread or misinterpreted their scriptures have caused most of the wars on this planet. That is why until the human race stops arguing over which path is truer, there will never be peace on Earth.

One of the problems with religion is that it usually only tells us what not to do. Yoga, on the other hand, teaches *how to be*. There is a current movement to place the Judeo-Christian ten "thou shalt nots" in American schools. Would it not be just as appropriate to put a list of things our children should do? To concentrate, be calm, be blissful? I am not suggesting either one. Yet, around 200 B.C., the Yoga adept Maharishi Patanjali codified a way to do the latter of the two. It has helped me immeasurably to understand myself, how to control anger, be calm and has only enhanced my religious beliefs and given me more clarity, not conflicted with them. It is easier said than done to declare, "love thy neighbor as thyself" or "do unto others as you would have them do unto you." Patanjali shows us in a relatively scientific way how to remove the obstacles that hinder us from following those simple teachings, as well as those of Buddha, Mohammad, Krishna, Moses and others in our daily lives.

A number of people have asked me, "How can you write a book about Yoga and not include pictures of you standing on your head?" My answer is a question. "How is showing you a picture of me standing on my head, sticking my foot behind my head, or performing some other advanced Hatha Yoga posture going to give you momentum on your path to Self-Realization and the achievement of Super-Conscious Bliss?" It might do just the opposite. You might think, I would never be able to do that in this lifetime and turn away, having never been exposed to what Yoga is really about.

Yoga Sutra 1.1 On Concentration leading to Samadhi or Supreme Contemplation:

> Atha=now, Yoga=of Yoga, Anushasanam=instruction
> 
> Now the exposition of Yoga and instruction into Yoga is made.

Patanjali's original discourse may have just been passed down verbally for centuries like Moses' Ten Commandments. I will assure you, however that if Patanjali's original text did exist today, it would not contain pictures of anatomically perfect models in leotards standing on their heads. There are hundreds of books about Yoga with beautifully sculpted models performing virtually the same 30 to 40 standard Hatha Yoga postures. If you buy one of these books and it is the cause of you becoming a Yoga Master, you will probably be the first. More than likely your "How to Do Yoga" book will end up in a yard sale, just another unfilled New Years resolution. The problem with these books is that the authors devote 90 percent of their effort to the physical postures, which are only one of the eight *equal* limbs, or parts, of Raja, or Ashtanga Yoga. The authors usually acknowledge the other seven limbs, or parts, of Raja Yoga in the last 10 percent of the book.

Please do not misinterpret me. It is not impossible to learn Yoga from a book, however lack of self-discipline is one of the major obstacles to Yoga and a good teacher is very important. Even a yoga teacher has a teacher or teachers to whom he/she returns for further guidance and instruction. Unfortunately, because of the way some Yoga classes are being taught many of the orthodox Yoga purists have openly complained that Yoga has degenerated into a physical fitness and beauty fad. An estimated 15 million Americans flock to fitness centers to practice the postures but very few would actually go to a meditation room. This can be attributed to our time-oriented society both on the part of students and teachers both who have other demands on their time. One example is a style of Yoga practice called "Power Yoga." Recent articles in *The Washington Post* and *The New York Times* have reported that the number of Yoga-related injuries has increased by an astronomical figure. Patanjali would roll in his grave if he knew that two thousand years after he codified Yoga Science people were being injured putting his teachings into practice. (He would roll in his grave, except for the fact that he was cremated in a funeral pyre and strongly believed in reincarnation.) (Similarly, I am sure that most people would agree that Christ and Mohammad would probably not be too thrilled to know that millions of people have been killed in their names by their followers, whose religious fervor was their pretext for violent acts.) Americans are largely of the opinion that if they have not sweated profusely in an exercise, they have not done anything positive for or to their bodies. They want results tomorrow although of course the physical condition in which they find themselves did not occur in a day. Athletes who take steroids or people who take pills to lose weight are a prime example of this attitude. Should you leave Yoga class breathing like you had to run to catch a bus, you missed the bus. You practiced aerobics or Pilates, not Yoga. The postures, should be performed slowly with absolute concentration on breath control, (pranayama the vital breath) Another teacher may disagree. No two people have the exact same perception of <u>any</u> projection from the outside world—Yoga included.

Another problem student's face is the investment in time and money that goes into practicing modern Yoga. The owners and teachers feel that they must cater to the wishes of the students for fear of losing them to another center or studio down the street. Meditation does not pay the bills. It is also very difficult for teachers in the southern United States to expose their students to the mental or spiritual aspects of Yoga, which are almost one in the same in so far as spirituality is a manifestation of the mind. I have even heard of some Yoga studios in the Bible belt region of the United States getting death threats because people in their community believe the occult is being propagated at their establishments. It is for this reason that a number of teachers in the southern United States encouraged me to write a book to help correct impressions of Yoga Science.

As I have previously stated, there are no pictures of me performing Hatha Yoga poses or postures like a billboard for a circus in this book. If I wanted to show you pictures of someone performing Yoga, I could have just as easily furnished pictures of the late Mother Theresa working in an orphanage in New Delhi, or a person handing out food in a homeless shelter, or anyone performing a selfless act. It is more important to perform selfless acts in order to ascend to another level of consciousness, than it is to stand on your head despite the many therapeutic values of doing so. These lessons are outlined in Patanjali's Sutras.

There are 840,000 Hatha yoga poses, or postures, and teachers did not develop most of them until 1,300 years after Patanjali codified Yoga Science. The teachers realized that the average human could not sit up straight for more than a limited amount of time to concentrate, meditate or contemplate God, Truth or the Self without getting a twitch in their neck, sore knees, pain in the back, etc. The general wisdom was that the body should be strengthened, straightened, then made flexible before the mind could begin to transcend to higher levels of consciousness.

This book is about the significantly large portion of Yoga to which you may not be exposed in a class, a book, or a video on the subject. There are 196 Sutras, or suggestions, that Patanjali elucidates in his Darsan, and only four mention the physical postures. So many of us Yogis believe that one cannot be a Yoga Practitioner by only practicing the physical postures. It is a package deal, Raja Yoga, the Royal Path. The postures are merely a first step, a vehicle to get you past the starting line on your *path* to Self-Realization.

If you did not notice, the title to this book is not "*The* Path to Super Conscious Bliss" but "*A* Path to Super Conscious Bliss." Patanjali's ideas and methods are universal, ecumenical and all encompassing. He denies no one and recommends techniques in only a scientific way. If you read this book and disagree with it or get nothing from it at all, that's fine, you must do what works for you. One technique that Patanjali suggests to maintain a calm mind is to never argue with anyone.

To calm your mind is the first step in Yoga.

(Please be aware that all the proceeds from this book will be donated to the World Peace Fund to help build wells in Third World Nations where two billion people do not have potable water. Even if this book ends up at a future yard sale, your money will have gone to a very worthy cause.)

Om, Shanti, Shanti, Shanti<br>
God, Peace, Peace, Peace

# PREFACE

The Yoga Sutras are also known as the Yoga Darsan (pronounced darshan) of Patanjali. Darsan has been defined literally as "an instrument of seeing." In his book *Beyond the Siddhi Powers*, John McAfee defined the word Sutra as "a string or line of thought". There are other teachers, such as mine, Dr. V.S. Rao, who have said it means literally a "thread or string on which each teacher puts their beads of experience to teach to a student"—much like a Catholic Rosary or Muslim prayer beads. It is for this reason that when someone translates an ancient language to me an alarm goes off in my head when they tell me a word or phrase *literally* means something. For example, a recent commentator defined the Sanskrit word "svarupe" as "in his own essence." My teacher and others define it as "in his own nature." That is why throughout this commentary I will use the term "has been defined," rather than "literally means." Because of my rudimentary knowledge of Sanskrit, I have chosen to use Dr. Rao's and Sri Sankara's translations of Sanskrit to English although there are as many similar translations of Sanskrit words into English, as there are major cities and provinces of India. It would obviously be neither practical nor useful to list them all.

When Christ, wanted to give a lesson to his disciples or to a gathering of the casual curious, he employed stories, allegories and analogies filled with metaphors known as parables. Someone once compiled all of these parables into a book. That book could have been entitled the "Darsan of Christ" or the "Sutras of Jesus." Why? How did Lord Christ come up with these parables? Reverend Father John Emmanuel Ridgell opined that "they were from his own life's experiences [and impressions of the outside world] that he meditated on"—His beads of experience. So too were Patanjali's. Both Christ's and Patanjali's lessons can be cryptic and not exactly to-the-point; both sets of lessons require concentration, meditation and contemplation to uncover their true meanings.

One of Christ's more familiar lessons is "It is easier for a camel to pass through the eye of a needle, than for a rich man to pass through the gates of Heaven." Some may ask, What is cryptic about that lesson? There are actually at least three lines of thought held by present-day Christians about what Christ meant by this statement. The first line of thought is that the "eye of a needle" was not a sewing needle but rather a colloquial term for a narrow gate to a field where sheep or goat herders communally kept their flocks, thus a camel could not pass through the gate unnoticed. The second line of thought is that the word "camel" was a colloquial term for a large rope, which would be hard to pass through the eye of a sewing needle. Then there is the third and obvious, more literal interpretation of a large animal passing through the eye of a sewing needle. Jesus' statement can be paraphrased, "Until you lose your attachments to the material world, your Soul will not be liberated," a belief that is similar to what Patanjali taught 200 years before Christ and also Buddha taught four hundred years before Patanjali. One may be reminded that both Christ, Patanjali and Buddha were addressing people who believed the world was flat. In Christ's lesson about the camel and the eye of a needle (to which I will refer in later chapters), He was metaphorically using objects familiar to his students to help them envision a seemingly impossible attainment. Using the most familiar line of thought, he employed the image of one of the largest animals known to his students.

Many Hindus have written commentaries on the Yoga Sutras; however the metaphors and analogies they use may not be objects or experiences with which Westerners, especially Americans, are familiar. So, at times, because of language and culture, there can be confusion in the meanings of lessons that they are trying to teach.

A case in point: Two Yoga students whom I met in St. Augustine, Florida, went to hear a Hindu Master give a lecture on Kaivalyam (Independence) and Cosmic Consciousness. The next day I asked them, what they learned?" The woman replied, "Wally fell asleep and I didn't understand a word he [the lecturer] said." Although the Hindu Master may have very well thought he was crystal clear on the subject matter of the lecture, the students came away empty-handed.

That is the other reason that I have undertaken this project. I hope the metaphors and analogies I use—my "beads of experience" so to speak—will be clearer to Westerners than those of Yoga masters with different cultural backgrounds. Most of my "beads" are in the first chapter and scattered throughout the last three chapters. As I pointed out earlier, all the translations of Sanskrit words are by Dr.

V.S. Rao and Sri Sankara except for one or two. These men and others have defined the word "chitta" or "citta" as "mind-stuff"-everything contained in or about the mind. When I was trying to explain chitta by referring to it as mind-stuff to a thirteen-year-old at my church, he amusingly informed me that he had never heard an adult use the word "stuff." So throughout this book I have used the term "mind-composite." I have also elaborated on words so that you will not go away from the book empty-handed or empty-minded.

Without further hesitation, I humbly and with great reverence present to you *A Christian Yogi's Commentary on the Yoga Darsan of Maharishi Patanjali, His Sutras.*

Namaste

"May the divine light in me greet and honor the divine light in you"

# MAHARISHI PATANJALI'S YOGA DARSAN

## CHAPTER I

# SAMADHI PADA—ON CONCENTRATION

1. Atha Yoganushasanam

Atha=now, Yoga=of yoga, Anushasanam=instruction

Now the exposition of Yoga and instruction into Yoga is made.

Dr. V. S. Rao wrote, "Patanjali is not only exposing Yoga philosophy but also direct instruction on how to practice Yoga since mere philosophy is not going to satisfy a seeker without direct experience of the supreme."

2. Yogah Chittah Vrutti Nirodah

Yogah=Yoga, Chitta=of the mind-composite, Vrutti=modifications, Nirodha=restraint

The restraint or hindrance of the modifications of the mind-composite is Yoga.

Yogis have compared our mind-composite to a lake. In its natural state it is placid, calm, without disturbances. The restraints we employ to keep certain mental waves from disturbing the mind-composite, or to prevent them from rising, is the ultimate goal of Yoga. The entire science of Yoga is based on these restraints. One has to join the body, mind and spirit in "union" to achieve this state and the experience of which is Yoga. It is indeed a fascinating experience.

In Yogic Science, the chitta (mind-composite) is the sum total of three different levels of the mind: the basic mind "Ahamkara"; the Ego or the feeling of "I," which gives rise to the "Buddhi," the intellect or discriminative faculty; and "Manas," the desiring part of the mind, which is attracted to outside objects through the senses.

There is a phenomenon known as "déja-vu," a feeling that one has previously experienced a situation he is in for the first time. Researchers believe it occurs when the eyes become out of sync for a period of time. One eye starts recording projections from the outside world as memory just a millisecond before the other eye records the same projection. The result is that, yes, you have a perception that you experienced, however, it was not weeks, months or years in the past but rather just milliseconds ago.

In comparison, Patanjali believed that our reactions to the outside world are caused by waves that act in succession from the three levels of the mind. This happens so quickly that we rarely distinguish between them.

Dr. Rao writes, [The entire outside world is based on our thoughts and mental attitude. The entire world is our own projection. Our values may change within a fraction of a second. Today you may not even want to see the one who was your sweet object of enjoyment yesterday. If we remember this, we won't put so much stress on outward things. That is why Yoga does not bother much about changing the outside world.]

> *Nothing exterior shall ever take command of me.*
>
> —Walt Whitman

"Man Eva Manushyanam bandha Mokshayoh"—'It is the mind, so the person." Bondage or liberation are manifestations of our own mental states. If you feel bound, you are bound. If you feel liberated, you are liberated. Things outside neither bind nor liberate you; only your attitude toward them does that. So if you can have control over the projections and change them as you want, you are not bound by the outside world. There is nothing wrong in God's creation in and of itself. You can make the world a heaven or hell based upon your approach and attitude. That is why the entire science of Yoga is based on Chitta Vrutti Nirodhah. If you control your mind, you have controlled everything and then there is nothing to bind you in this world.

When the waves disturb the placid lake, of your mind-composite those waves, called Vrittis, cloud and muddy the waters of your mind and prevent you from seeing the bottom, which can be thought of as your own Self. When the lake is clear and there are no waves, then and only then will you see your own true Self.

Patanajli states that the mind has three states. The first is Tamas, or darkness. It is found prevalent in tyrants, bullies and it only acts to injure. Then there is Rajas, the active state of mind, the chief motives of which are power and enjoyment. Lastly there is Sattva, the state of serenity or tranquility, in which the mind is calm. Contrary to the way it sounds, this state is not inactive but rather extremely active. It takes great power to remain calm in a situation. In a speeding car going downhill it takes a strong person to apply the brakes; a weaker person would let it continue out of control. A calm person is neither dull nor lazy. A calm person has control. The mind-composite is always trying to move toward the calm state but the sense organs bring it out of that calmness. To be calm is the first step in Yoga.

> *The disciplined man masters thoughts by stillness and emotions by calmness.*
>
> —Lao-Tzu

According to Yogic Science the mind will manifest into five states, from a less developed state to the highest. How this occurs is explained in more detail in Chapter Three.

"Ragas" are things we like, and "Dweshas" are things we dislike, in between those likes and dislikes are attraction and repulsion, virtue and vice, knowledge and ignorance, rich and poor. These are characteristics of "Kshipta Chitta" (a darkening mind) which is dull and tends to injure.

"Kama" (lust), "Krodha" (anger), "Lobha" (greed), and "Moha" (delusion or infatuation), will manifest as "Mudha" (or a scattering mind). A scattering mind, when active, has a tendency to move toward pleasure and pain. It can lead to sleep, dullness, fear, laziness, and dependence as a result of "Tamoguna", which is also explained in more detail in Chapter Three.

"Karma" leads to "Vikshipta Chipta" (a gathering mind), which leads one to become virtuous, knowledgeable and prosperous.

"Sattva Guna" is the continuous flow of thought on one luminous idea, which leads to "Ekagrata Chitta" (a Yogic one-pointed mind) that allows the mind to obtain purity and tranquility. In this state, the mind will become crystal-clear, all-knowing and discriminating.

"VivekaKhyathi" is the discrimination that leads to "Nirudha Chita (a concentrating mind), after which the mind becomes identified with the Supreme Spirit, which is the goal of many Yoga Practitioners.

3. Tada Drastuh Svarupe Vasthanam

Tada=then, Drastuh=the seer, Svarupe=in His own nature, Avasthanam=abides

Then the Seer (Self) abides in His own nature.

Everyone has displayed fits of anger to a stranger, acquaintance or even a loved one at some time in their life. (According to Scriptural Testimony in the New Testament to the Bible, Jesus kicked over the tables of some moneychangers and whipped the men outside his Father's house of worship). After one's mind returns to a calmer state, one may reflect upon one's behavior and apologize, saying, "I'm sorry, I wasn't myself." At that moment, the Seer (Self) is the real you having stepped back to see what your mind itself had done. After a restraint has been employed to calm the waves of the mind-lake, the mind will re-attain a natural blissful state; which is its own nature.

The next 192 Sutras give you suggestions on how to accomplish what was contained in the previous two.

4. Vrutti Sarupyam Itaratra

Vrutti=modifications of the mind-composite, Sarupyam=assumes the form, Itaratra=at other times

At other times than concentration, the seer (self) is identified with the modifications.

In an opposite scenario, you may be the target of someone's verbal abuse. He/she may call you fat, stupid, ugly, or poor. Would that disturb you? Yes, of course. But what produced the modification that disturbed your mind? Your mind produced the modification. There is great wisdom in the children's rhyme, "Sticks and stones may break my bones but words can never hurt me." We forget these words of wisdom as we grow older. *You* produce the modification or wave that disturbs your mind lake. *You* lose your real identity and start identifying with your thoughts and body. If you say, "I am fat," you have identified yourself with an overweight body. If you say, "I am poor," you are identifying yourself with numbers in a bank account. Dr. Rao writes, [If you detach yourself completely from all the things you have identified yourself with, you realize yourself as the pure 'I am'. In that 'I' state there will be no difference between you and me.] In short we are all the same, only in different physical forms.

5. Vruttahya Panchatayah Klishta Aklishtah

Vruttahya=Modification of the mind-composite, Panchatayyah=five kinds, Klishta=painful (selfish thoughts), Aklishtah=painless (selfless thoughts).

There are five kinds of mental modifications, which can be either painful or painless.

Maharishi Patanjali says there are five kinds of Vruttis (modifications) that are grouped into two categories. One variety brings pain; the other does not. He did not divide them into painful and pleasurable. The reason being that even a so-called pleasurable thought may ultimately bring pain. We never know in the beginning whether or not a particular thought will bring pain. Some thoughts begin as painful but end up leaving us at peace. Others appear at first to be pleasurable but bring pain. Selfish thoughts ultimately bring pain. Dr. Rao wrote, [To love something or somebody is pleasurable, but in the end brings lots of pain, hatred, jealousy and unhappiness if that love was not a pure love but was based on some expectation in return. Thus there was selfishness in that love. With such expectations, love seldom lasts long. So love, though it appears to be a painless thought, ultimately ends in pain if it is based on selfishness.]

In a different situation, a feeling of anger that a teacher directs toward a student, might bring pain to the student in the beginning but end up being beneficial as the student corrects his/her folly. Thus the anger of a selfless person, like a teacher, has no personal motive behind it; it only serves to help and correct his/her student. Whatever the thought is, if there is no selfishness behind it, it can never really bring pain to the person concerned. The result is neither pain nor pleasure but peace.

*The roots of education are bitter, but the fruit is sweet.*

—Aristotle

Patanjali suggests we should, analyze all motives and try to cultivate selfless thoughts. The analysis of which thoughts are selfish and which are not, is Yoga in practice.

Patanjali now names the five types of modifications (Vrittis) and explains them.

6. Pramana Viparya Vilalpa Nidra Smrutayah

Pramana=right or correct knowledge, Viparya=misconception
Vikalpa=verbal delusions, Nidra=sleep, Smrutayah=memory

Right or correct knowledge, misconception, verbal delusions, sleep, memory.

He now describes them in more detail.

7. Pratyaksha Anummana Agamah Pramanani

Pratyaksha=direct perception, Anummana=inference, Agamah=Scriptural testimony, Pramanani=are the source of right knowledge

The sources of right or correct knowledge are direct perception, inference and scriptural testimony.

If you were to see someone die in front of you, that tragic event would create a wave that would disturb you. In a quite different scenario, if you were to receive notice that you had won a lottery or a Publisher's Clearinghouse Sweepstakes, that news would also create a wave that would leave you less than calm. You directly perceived both events, painful and painless.

If you came up to your home and saw smoke rising behind it, you would likely think that your house was on fire. Although you would not see a fire, you inferred that there was one. This inference would create a wave that would disturb you. Inference is proof, although not a fact, and it is right knowledge.

If a reliable authority—for example a prophet or saint for instance—tells you something about a subject about which he/she is very knowledgeable

—like Holy Scripture—this is also right knowledge.

If two perceptions do not contradict each other it is a case of proof. Direct perception, inference and the words of the great are sources of right knowledge.

8. Viparyayo Mithyajnamam Atadrupa Pratishtam

Viviparyayo=misconception is, Mithyajmanam=false knowledge, atadrupa=not on that form, Pratishtham=based

A misconception is knowing the unreal having a form not its own.

If you walked into your home and saw your significant other embracing another person whose back was to you, you might initially feel jealousy. However, if the person turned around and revealed himself or herself to be a sibling or relative, you would feel differently. A favorite Indian example of misperception is that of a fear of a coiled rope that *looks* like a snake. The fear is real, the snake is not. Erroneous impressions can create disturbing waves as well as correct, or right, knowledge.

9. Shabdajmananupati Vasu Sunyo Vikalpah

Shabdjmana=knowledge on words, Anupati=arises, Vasu=reality Sunyo=without any, vikalpah=verbal delusion

If someone lies to you or about you it creates an image without basis in reality. A polite but convoluted way of saying you do not believe someone is, "I'm sorry but you've created a verbal delusion; there is no corresponding reality to what you have just said." With a misconception, there is physical evidence contributing to the misperception, but in a Vikalpah there are nothing but the thoughts or illusions they create.

10. Abhava Pratyayalambana Vrittir Nidra

Abhava=nothingness, Pratayaya=cognition, Alambana=support, vrittir=modification of mind, Nidra=sleep

That mental modification supported by cognition of nothingness is sleep.

Dr. Rao writes, [In the waking state you know that you have been sleeping and you will have only the memory of perception. That which you do not perceive, you never can have any memory of. Normally, we say we do not have any thought in the mind during sleep. But actually we have a thought, that is why when we wake up we say, 'I slept very well, I knew nothing.' You know nothing, but you know that you know that you know nothing. Don't think there is no thought in sleep. Every reaction is a ripple on the lake of the mind. So, if during sleep the mind has no ripples, it would have no perception, positive or negative and we would not remember them. The very reason of our remembering sleep is that during sleep there was a certain class of waves in the mind. We are experiencing a dream in sleep and we remember that too. If there were no thought and you were completely unconscious, you would not even feel that you had slept. All other thoughts are temporarily suspended except this one thought of emptiness in mind, which leaves its impression upon waking.]

Researchers have discovered that even in sleep there is what is called Rapid Eye Movement. While dreaming your eyes will move as if you are watching a live event. You can experience terror or pleasure in sleep—painless and painful sleep.

11. Anubhuta Vishayasampramoshah Smritih

Anubuhta=experienced, Vishaya=objects, Asampranoshah=not forgotten, smrithih=memory

Memories, good or bad, of direct perceptions, inferences and verbal delusions will manifest themselves to disturb you even if you do not want them to.

Dr. Rao writes, [Memory is the retaining of the mental impressions of an object without loss. When a mental modification of an object previously experienced and not forgotten comes back to consciousness that is memory.]

A word is just like a stone thrown in to the lake of mind-composite; it causes a wave, which in turn arouses a series of waves; and this series is memory. The same is true in sleep. When a particular kind of wave, which we call sleep, throws the mind-composite into a wave of memory; it is called a dream. A dream is another form of the wave, which in the waking state is called memory.

Dr. Rao writes, [Memories create impressions in the mind that at a later time come to the surface, either when we want them to or sometimes even when we do not want them to. Memories come in two ways: dreams are memories that come to surface when we sleep; daydreams are memories that arise during the day. Both are impressions which, when formed, slowly descend to the bottom of the mind and come to the surface when they are rekindled for some reason or other.] Often some unknown trigger causes this.

Patanjali described the five kinds of "Vrittis," or thought forms, that must be controlled to make the mind pure and to allow inner peace to shine through. In the following Sutras he explains how to control them. As I pointed out in the Preface, these lessons have been handed down in both written and verbal form for over 2,000 years. The commentaries on the Yoga Sutras are generally commentaries on commentaries; one part of a chain of commentaries that will go on *ad infinitum.* Each teacher adds a few of his/her own "beads of experience". I have modified a thousand words of my teacher in hopes of making the message easier for you to understand. I have also added my own beads. As a Registered Yoga Alliance Teacher I am obliged to remove any obstacles to your path of attaining Absolute Oneness with the Infinite Supreme Being. Those obstacles may be language, culture or religious beliefs.

12. Abhysa Vairagyabhyam Tannirodhah

Abhysa=by practice, Vairagyabhyam=by non-attachment
Tannirodhah=they are restrained

To have non-attachment the mind must be clear, good and rational.

Actions and feelings are like pulsations on the surface of the mind-lake. Even though the vibrations die out, the impressions remain. When a large number of these impressions remain on the mind, they begin to coalesce into a habit. When the impressions left by these vibrations pass out of the mind, each one leaves a mark. The mark <u>is</u> the result. Our character is the sum total of these marks; it depends on the tone of the waves that prevail. If good prevails, one becomes good; if bad prevails, one becomes bad; if joy prevails; one becomes happy and so on. The only remedy for bad habits is good counter habits. Bad habits are controlled by good habits. Keep performing good deeds and thinking holy thoughts, and you can suppress the bad habits. Character develops from repeated habits, and repeated good habits alone reform character.

On the positive side, you should practice any good habit. Alternately, you can detach yourself from the cause that create bad habits. Patanjali gives both a positive and negative approach to thought control, which he elucidates in the following Sutras.

13. Tatr Sthitau Yatnabyasah

Tatr=of these, Sthitau=steadiness, Yatnah=effort, Bhyasah=practice

Of these two, effort towards steadiness of the mind is practice.

Continuous struggle to keep the modifications perfectly maintained involves practice. The attempt to restrain the mind in Chitta form, to prevent the forming of these waves, is Yoga. Merely practicing the physical postures alone cannot prevent these waves from forming. This Sutra means not allowing your mind to have free time to create the waves. It means scrutinizing every thought, every word and every feeling and action.

*Practice is the best of all instructions.*

—Aristotle

14. Sa Tu Dirgha Kala Nairantarya Satkarasevito Dhrudhabhumih

Sah=this, Tu=and, Dirgha=long, Kala=time, Nairantarya=without break, Satkara=earnestness, Asevitah=well attended to, Dridhabhumih=firm ground

Practice becomes firmly grounded (established) when well attended to for a long time, without break and in all earnestness. It becomes firmly grounded by long and constant effort, with great love for the end to be obtained. Restraint is not achieved in one day, but with long term continuous practice. We always need practice, devotion and faith to achieve success in Yoga.

15. Dristanusravika Vishaya Vitrushasya Vairagyam

Drishta=Seen, Anusravika=hear, Vishaya=object, Vitrishnasya=consciousness, Vairagyam=non-attachment

Non-attachment is that effort which comes to those who have given up their thirst for objects either seen or heard; a thirst which wills to control those objects. The self-mastery in one that is free from craving for objects they have seen or even objects they have heard about is dispassion or non-attachment.

Dr. Rao writes, [Normally the mind gets attached by seeing or hearing something. It is mainly through the eyes and ears that the mind goes out and gathers things to satisfy its desires.]

16. Tat Param Purusha Khyater Guna Vaitrushnyam

Tat=that, Param=supreme, Purusha=true Self, Khyater=due to the realization, Guna=constituents of Nature, Vaitrushnyam=non-thirst

In an extreme form of non-attachment, one gives up everything but his essential properties. It comes about from the knowledge of the real nature of the Purusha that has been defined in this context as the true self. (It is later defined as the Supreme Soul). When there is no-thirst for even the Gunas (everything of nature), due to a realization of the Purusha (true self) that is supreme non-attachment. Recall Christ's lesson, "It is easier for a camel to pass through the eye of a needle than for a rich man to pass through the gates of Heaven." In this Sutra, Patanjali says one's soul will not be liberated until he gives up his material attachments, a teaching similar in meaning to Christ's needle analogy.

Many commentators go a little deeper by explaining a different form of attachment such as; mental attachments, like bad habits. Patanjali explains a higher form of what is called Vairagya. To put in constraints, to stop your mind from creating new bad habits is the ordinary Vairagya. There will always be new things to tempt you. Is it possible for the mind to have no desires? Patanjali says no, because the mind was made to desire.

However, one may ask, what about old bad habits that are still left as impressions? They could become manifest, like weeds that have been cut and not uprooted. Someone who has used drugs, smoked cigarettes and abused alcohol still retain the memory of those things. He might feel great that he no longer engages in those destructive behaviors, but the memory remains of the pleasure he had while doing it.

Those memories will only be erased when he succeeds in going within himself realizing the peace and joy of his own true Self. Dr. Rao writes, [The moment you understand yourself as the true Self, you find such peace and bliss, that the impressions of the petty enjoyments you experienced before, become as ordinary specks of light in front of the brilliant sun. You lose all interest in them permanently.]

A passage in the "Isavasya Upanishad" reads, [Keep the heart in God and the head in the world. If you know how to put your heart in God, you can rest there always, and still play in the world. Only when you have found the source and connected one part of the mind there, then you can enjoy everything.]

In the Sutras there are many references to the Hindu name for God (Isvara), and Prana (the vital life force or vital breath). Christians and anyone else should realize that it is not necessary to become Hindu, Buddhist or to join any particular religion in order to practice Yoga. The reason I raise this point again is that in the last ten Yoga classes I have attended in three different states, 85 percent of the students had Judeo-Christian backgrounds. Some of what is contained in the next 180 Sutras, or suggestions, might create a Vritti or modification to the mind-lake of some Judeo-Christians. Why? They may come across as verbal delusions, words that to a Judeo-Christian have no corresponding reality. Keep an open mind. You may find out that what Patanjali suggests to you, was not meant to change your mind about your own personal religious beliefs, but rather to help you to achieve your ultimate goal. It is practical and based on scientific evidence.

17. Vitarka Vichara Ananda Asmita Anugamat Samprajnatah

Vitarka=reasoning, Vichara=reflecting, Ananda=rejoicing, Asmita=pure ego, Anugamat=accompanied by the forms of, Samprajnatah=distinguished

Samprajnata Samadhi is distinguished contemplation. Samadhi is contemplation, the final goal of Yoga. Reasoning, reflecting, rejoicing and pure I-am-ness accompany Samprajanata Samadhi. This concentration is called right knowledge and is followed by reasoning, discrimination, bliss and unqualified egoism.

Patanjali explains the theory of Yoga and then discusses the final practice called Samadhi and its variations. In this and the following Sutras, Patanjali discusses two varieties of Samadhis: Samprajanata (distinguished), and Asamprajnata, (undistinguished). He further divides the Samprajanata Samadhi into four forms. To understand them, we have to understand the composition of what he calls nature, or Prakruti, which has four divisions: gross material; subtle elements which are called the Tanmatras which ultimately express the concrete forms you see; the mind-composite Chittam; and the ego, or individuality.

You must first practice on the gross objects, Savitarka, then on the subtle elements, Savichara, then on the mind, Sa-Ananda, and finally on the "I" feeling alone, Sa-Asmita. There has to be a gradation because we cannot immediately contemplate that which is very subtle.

You must first train your mind to focus on something concrete. When the mind is fully focused on a concrete object; that is called Savitarka Samadhi. Remember that at this point the mind is already well under control. The moment the fully focused mind contemplates an object, it penetrates to the very depth of that object and understands every particle of it. A focused mind gains power, and when that powerful mind concentrates on an object the entire knowledge of that object is revealed to it.

The focused mind then contemplates the Tanmatras, or subtle elements. Here there is no concrete object to see. You contemplate something abstract like love. With abstract concepts like love, for example, a normal person cannot understand it without the help of a concrete object. But if the focused mind contemplates and understands the concrete objects well, then it will rise above time and space also. This Samadhi is called Savichara, with reflection.

In the fourth Samadhi, not even Ananda (rejoicing) is there, just awareness of the Self. The mind is just there, and it is aware of nothing else. This is called Sa-Asmita Samadhi, "with ego". It may not be possible to visualize what that could be, but still, try to understand it theoretically at least. In Sa-Asmita Samadhi, the Samskaras (past memories) are in the mind in their seed form. Even though we are only aware of "I am," the impressions (past memories, pleasant and unpleasant) are still buried in the mind. Thus the Samprajanata Samadhis are a process of going inward—not evolution, but involution. Originally the world or Prakruti is said to be un-manifested. When it begins to manifest, Ahamkara (ego) comes first; then the individuality emerges and last, the mind from which the Tanmatras and the gross elements are manifested, the process is called natural evolution. In Yogic meditation we experience involution.

Patanjali is completely scientific in this respect. He sees Yoga as a rigorous science and never hesitates to explain all aspects of the practice and its ramifications.

Unless we understand Prakruti (nature), very well, we cannot just leave it. We cannot just ignore it or set it aside. That is why the Samprajnata samadhis are to be practiced first, one after the other.

Dr. Rao writes, [But there is a danger in Samprajnata Samadhi also. It is to be practiced, but we have to face the danger also. That is why we have to prepare ourselves with purity and selflessness. Otherwise, we will be in danger with our new found powers.]

> 18. Virama Pratyayabhyasa Pruvah Samskarasheshah Anyah.
>
> Virama=complete cessation, Pratyaya=firmly convinced, Abhyasapurva=by the practice, Samsharasheshah=having only the impressions remain, Anyah=the other
>
> By the firmly convinced practice of the complete cessation of the mental modifications, only the impressions remain. This is the other Samadhi, Asamprajnata or non-distinguished.

In the state of Samprajnata Samadhi the buried seeds will still come into the conscious mind when the proper opportunity arises, and will eventually drag us into some worldly experience. That is why, after all these four stages have been passed through, you will attain the state of Asamprajanata Samadhi where even the ego feeling is not there and the seeds of the past impressions are rendered harmless. In that state, only the consciousness is there—nothing else. Once that is achieved, the individual is completely liberated and his past impressions will no longer affect him. Although you appear to be in the world, you are not actually involved in it.

This is Jivanmukta the state of one who lives but at the same time is liberated and free. This is what is known as the perfect super-conscious state, Asamprajanata Samadhi, the state that gives freedom. The Samprajanata Samadhis will not give freedom. You may obtain a number of powers in the state of meditation, only to fall back down again. There is no safeguard against this fall until the soul transcends nature. It is very difficult to achieve Asamprajanata Samadhi, even though the method to achieve it seems easy. The method is to meditate on the mind itself, and whenever a thought arises, to strike it down, allowing no thought to come into the mind, thus making it like a vacuum. If you can do this, at that very moment you shall attain liberation. To be able to really do this is to manifest the greatest strength, the greatest control. When this state is reached, the Samadhi becomes "seedless." When during concentration there is consciousness where the mind succeeds in only quelling the waves in the mind-composite in which they only hold them down, the waves, however, remain in the form of tendencies, seeds, which may become waves in time. When all the internal tendencies are destroyed, thereby almost destroying the mind, the Samadhi becomes "seedless"; and at that level, there are no more seeds to produce again and again in this plant of life, this ceaseless round of birth and death. In this state there is no mind, no knowledge. Both good and evil tendencies will suppress each other in this state, leaving alone the Soul, in its own splendor and glory, unaffected by good and bad, and it remains as the Omnipresent, Omnipotent and Omniscient Lord of the Universe.

19. Bhavapratyayo Videha Prakrutilayanam

Bhavapratyayo=birth is caused, Videha=bodies physically dead, Prakrutilayanam=merged in nature

After the bodies of the physically dead are merged in nature, birth is caused.

This is the part where Christians and Hebrews start scratching their heads. If you believe that Heaven is where we all sit around on fluffy clouds listening to harp music, remembering all the petty enjoyments we enjoyed on earth, you may be lost here. If you can imagine that we might have to polish up our souls during each life before sitting at the "hand of the Father" or becoming immersed in the Supreme Soul, at least try to understand this Sutra theoretically from the Yogic and/or Hindu perspective.

Suppose you have practiced some Yoga; you've learned the lotus position, learned to regulate your breath, learned a little mantra repetition and learned to relax. When you die, will all of that have been a waste? Patanjali says no. Whatever you gained in this life will go with you into the next, and you will be closer to liberation than if you never were exposed to Yoga (or some sort of spirituality) in this life.

Then again, you might get pulled back into the desires and attachments that keep you from Perfection again and again. Someone asked me, "What do you think you were in a past life?" I told them, it did not matter to me, and the only thing that mattered was that this be my last life. I want to get it right this time. Time is short and knowledge is infinite.

So Christians should not worry about reincarnation being absent from their Holy Scriptures. Get it right this time and it will be a moot point. You will not have to come back. Try to attain Asamprajnata Samadhi and you might eliminate the need of another rebirth.

20. Sraddha Virya Smriti Samadhi Prajna Purvaka Itaresham

Sraddha=faith, Virya=Strength, Smriti=memory, Samadhi=contemplation, Prajna Purvaka=or by discernment, Itaresham=for the others

To the others, this Asmprajnata Samadhi could come through faith, strength, memory, and contemplation or by discernment.

21. Tivara Samvegenam Asahhah

Tivara=keen, Samvegenam=intent, Asahhah=practice

This Samadhi will come very quickly with keen and intent practice.

22. Mruda Madhyadhimatratvat Tatopi Visheshah

Mruda=mild, Madhya=medium, Adhimatratvat=intense, Tatopi=further, Visheshah=differentiation

The time necessary for success further depends on whether the practice is mild, medium or intense.

23. Isvara Pranihanatva

Isvara=God, Pranihanat=dedicated devotion, va=or

Here, Patanjali says that there is another way to achieve success. It is by self-surrender to Isvara, who is nothing but Supreme Consciousness, not the individual soul but the Supreme Soul. He goes on to further explain who or what Isvara is. His definition of the Supreme Being or the Supreme Consciousness does not deviate from what any major religion's definition is of such a being. Isvara is just another name. The general consensus is that there is only one Infinite Supreme Being. How could there be two or more Beings that are Infinite? In my daily life I do not refer to God as Isvara. I do not refer to the Infinite Supreme Being as Allah except when I am in conversation with a Muslim. Whatever your religious beliefs are, however, see if the definitions below describe your deity or concept of the Infinite Supreme Being.

24. Klesha Karma Vipaka Ashayair Aparamrushta Purusahvisheshah

Klesha=afflictions, Karma=actions, vipaka=fruit of actions, Ashayair=impressions of desire, Aparamrushtah=unaffected by, Purusha=supreme soul, Isvarah=God

Isvara is the Supreme Purusha, unaffected by any afflictions, actions, and fruits of desire or by any inner impressions of desire.

25. Tatra Nirathishayam Sarvajna Bijam

Tatra=in him, Nirathishayam=complete manifestation, Sarvajna=omniscience, Bijam=seed

Dr. Rao writes, [In Him is the complete manifestation of the seed of omniscience. In other words, He is all knowing. He is knowledge itself. The cosmic knowledge is called the supreme soul or Purusha. How can we imagine or visualize? Imagine a circle. We see space inside it and outside it. The inner space is finite and the outer is an infinite one. Without infinite there cannot be finite. The thought of one implies the other. We feel that our minds and knowledge are limited and finite. So, there must be a source of infinite knowledge beyond that.]

26. Sa Esha Purveshamampi Guruh Kalenanavachchedat.

Sa=He, Esha=this, Purveshamampi=even of the ancients, Guruh=teachers=Kalena=by time,=anavachchedat=unconditioned

Unconditioned by time, He is the teacher of even the most ancient teachers.

Dr. Rao writes, [Even though all knowledge is within us and we need not get it from outside, yet, somebody is still necessary to help us understand our own knowledge.]

That is why a teacher, Guru, Priest, Rabbi etc. is necessary. She/He helps us go within and understand ourselves.

All knowledge has been passed down since the beginning of human existence. Every priest had a priest. Every rabbi had a rabbi, and every Yoga teacher had a Yoga teacher—an endless chain of teachers back to the source, the all knowing.

27. Taya Vachaka Pranavah

Taya=of Isvara, Vachaka=word expressive, Pranavah=mystic sound or humming

"OM"

The word expressive of Isvara is the mystic sound "Om". Om is God's name as well as form.

Om appears in the "Upanishads," the Hindu attempt at defining the infinite by the finite; the import or meaning of every known religion through its scripture. The Latin word for "all" is Omne. They both mean omniscient, omnipotent and omnipresent; or, God. It is hard to know who started the practice of humming God's name, however many Yoga practitioners give Patanjali credit. It is pronounced as one continuous "ah oh mmm" and is spelled AUM. Pranavah has been defined as "humming." As it has been told to me, Patanjali wanted to give Isvara a name that was not so limited. Even God is limited because the letters are limited. Patanjali wanted a name that was unlimited in structure, and included all vibrations, sounds and syllables, because God is like that, infinite. Of the three letters, "A" represents manifestation, "U" represents maintenance and "M" stands for dissolution. I have a number of Mantras I use, but OM is like Supreme music everywhere eternally. It replaces whatever impure thought I might have with God's love. I have other mantras I use, such as "Hail Mary, Mother of God" or even Psalms like "In my soul stillness waits", or "Shepherd me O God." They are for certain occasions or situations in which I find myself. People of all religious faiths should not be afraid of chanting or humming OM. It is simply God's name.

28. Tajjapas Tadartha Bhavanam.

Tat=that, Japah=to repeat, Tat=that, Artha=meaning, Bhavananam=reflection

The repetition of Om and meditating on its meaning is another way to Samadhi. To repeat it with reflection upon the actual meaning is an aid.

When you repeat and reflect on Om and its actual meaning, the mind-composite becomes single-pointed. This is Japa Yoga, communion with God by repeating His name. By repeating his name constantly, a part of your mind moves towards Him; a part of your consciousness is tied to God through your Mantra, while the other part is still active in this world. Dr. Rao writes, [What you repeat and think, that you will become. So, that is why the right name which is holy and elevates our mind, should be taken as a Mantra. It is a very powerful technique, but the easiest, simplest and the best.]

29. Tata Pratyak Chetana Dhigamopyantaryabhavas chas.

Tat=from this, Pratyak=inner, Chetana=Self, Adigamah=knowledge, Opy=also, Antaraya=obstacles, Abhavah=disappear, Cha=and

Dr. Rao writes, [From this practice all the obstacles disappear and simultaneously dawns knowledge of the inner Self. You get in tune with cosmic power and you feel that force in you, imbibe all those qualities, get the cosmic vision, transcend all limitations and become that transcendental reality. Mind and body limit you, but by holding something infinite you slowly raise yourself from the finite objects that bind you and transcend them. Through that you get rid of all the obstacles and your path is made easy.]

Patanjali describes the obstacles in the following Sutras.

30. Vyadhi Styana Samshaya Pramada Alasya Avirati Bhranti-Darsana Alabdha-Bhumikatva Anavasthutatvani Chitta Viksepah TeAntharayah

Vyadhi=disease, Styana=dullness, Samsheya=doubt, Pramada=carelessness, Alasya Avirati=sensuality, Bhranti-darsana=false perception, Alabvha-bhumikatvam=slipping down from the ground gained, Anavasthutatvani=failure to reach firm ground, Chtta vikshepah=distractions of the mind-composite, Te=these, Antarayah=obstacles

Disease, dullness, doubt, carelessness, laziness, sensuality, false perception, failure to reach firm ground and slipping from the ground gained are the distractions of the mind-composite and obstacles.

31. Duhka Daurmanasya Angamejayatva Savasa Prasvasa Vikshepa Sahabhuvah

Duhkha=distress, Daurmanasya=despair, Angamejayatva=trembling of the body, Savasa=disturbed inhalation, Pravsasa=disturbed exhalation, Vikshepa=mental distraction, Sahabhuvah=accompaniments

Accompaniments to the mental distractions include distress, despair, trembling of the body and disturbed breathing.

Dr. Rao writes, [These are symptoms that we all sometimes experience which prevent concentration and meditation. That is why we have to take care of our day-to-day activities, movements, associations and diet. We should not allow our body and mind to be Tamasic. They should always be in a Sattvic or tranquil condition. That cannot be created all of a sudden by meditation alone, so we have to take care of all these things in our daily life. A sickly body can never be fit to sit, it will not allow the mind to meditate quietly.]

Weak nerves will at times create tremors. Occasionally, a person meditates they will tremble and perspire when he/she meditates. These are symptoms of physical weakness. But such things will not happen if he/she keeps his body in proper condition through right diet, exercise, and rest and does not allow it to be lazy and dull. Concentration brings perfect repose to mind and body. Repetition of Om and self-surrender to God will bring fresh energy to the mind.

32. Tat Pratishedha Ardham Eka-Tattvabhyasah

Tat=their, Pratishedha=prevention, Ardham=for, Eke=single, Tattva=subject, Abhyasah=practice

Maybe you are not ready to chant Om. Concentrate on a spot on the floor, the center of a Star of David, the center of a cross, a candle or any single subject that will bring your mind to a single-pointed concentration. However; after time, you may come to realize that chanting or humming God's name whether in Sanskrit or one of 3,000 other languages is the only thing that will overcome *all* distractions. You do not have to speak perfect Sanskrit to practice Yoga any more than you have speak perfect Latin to be a Roman Catholic. Protestants sing the beautiful piece of music "Ave Maria" in Latin by because it flows more beautifully in the language in which it was written and originally performed. Gregorian chant can be quite calming to people who do not understand Latin. Try Om (Aum), it is the sound current, the stream of life and it flows in Sanskrit or Omne if you are Catholic or Protestant. If not as Patanjali always said, do what works for you. Patanjali's teachings are all merely suggestions. No true Yogi will argue with you because it will disturb the mind. In the following Sutras Patanjali provides suggestions for attaining and maintaining one-pointedness. He does not try to squeeze us into one path.

33. Maitri Karuna Mudetopekshanam Suksha Duksha Punya Vishayanam Bhavanatah Chitta Prasadadanam

Maitri=Friendliness, Karuna=compassion, Mudita=delight, passion Upekshaman=disregard, Suksha=happy, Duksha=unhappy, Punya=virtuous, Apunya=wicked, Vishayanam=in the case of, Bhavanatah=by cultivating attidudes, Chitta=mind-composite, Prasadanam=undisturbed calmness

By cultivating attitudes of friendliness toward the happy, compassion for the unhappy, delight in the virtuous and disregard toward the wicked, the mind-composite retains its undisturbed calmness.

Dr. Rao wrote, [If we follow this Sutra, we will have the ability to keep a peaceful mind in our daily life. Everybody wants to have serenity of mind and likes to be happy always.] Patanjali provides four tools: friendliness, compassion, delight and disregard. There are only four kinds of persons in the world: they are happy, unhappy, virtuous and wicked (indifferent). By using Patanjali's four tools we will be able to properly deal with each type of person. If you come across happy people be friendly with them. If you happen to be with the unhappy, use the tool of kindness and be compassionate to them. If you are in the company of virtuous people be delighted. Lastly if you chance to come across wicked people, just go the other way. If you keep these four tools with you, you will be happy and always maintain serenity and calmness of the mind.

Five of the next six transliterations begin with word "or" which may seem grammatically incorrect at first glance. The reason for that is if the transliterations and following commentaries were removed from the next six Sutras, the sentences could all be contained in one paragraph. For instance; if someone asked me how to get from the West coast of the United States to the East coast, my reply might be; well you could go this way, or this way, or this, way etc. Those instructions may not explicit enough to keep you from getting lost.

34. Pracchardana Vidharanabhyam Va Pranasya

Pracchardana=exhalation, Vidharanabhyam=and by retention, Va=or, Pranasya=of the breath

Or that calmness is retained by the controlled exhalation or retention of the breath.

A psychologist will tell you that whenever you are agitated, worried or puzzled, you should take a few deep breaths, concentrating your entire mind on the breath. Within a few minutes you will find that your mind is calmer and more serene. This practice was in fact developed by Yogi's over thousand of years and is called Pranayama.

In Hawaii, the greeting the Islanders use is "Aloha" that has been defined as "may the breath of life be with you." Prana has been defined both as "vital breath" and also "life breath." Some Christians forget that another term for the Holy Spirit is "the breath of Life." After reading the definition of "Prana" below (compiled from many Yoga Masters) Christians may see a direct connection between Prana and the Holy Spirit. It is my personal belief that if there is a difference it is inconsequential, in short they are one and the same.

Prana is not exactly breath. It is the name for the energy that is in the universe. Whatever is seen in the universe, whatever moves or works or has life; is a manifestation of this Prana. The sum total of energy displayed in the universe is called Prana. It manifests as nervous motion in animals and plants, as thought in human beings, and in the physical universe as electricity, gravitation, repulsion, sound, and light. The whole universe is a combination of Prana and Akasha (ether of space). Out of Akasha the different materials that can be felt and seen are evolved, and out of Prana all the various forces. A leaf on a tree is not Prana; the force or energy that causes it to manifest is Prana. Now this throwing out-and restraining the Prana is what is called Pranayama. By expulsion and retention of breath, obstacles are overcome and the mind becomes peaceful, happy, serene and stable.

You should always remember that the mind and Prana, have close connections. Where the mind goes, the Prana follows. If you hit your knee, you hold your breath while holding the injury. If your mind is agitated, you will breathe heavily. If you pick up something heavy, you may hold your breath while straining. If you are deeply interested in reading something and break the concentration to watch your breath, you will notice that you are hardly breathing at all. When your mind is concentrated and still, the breath stops. So in the reverse way, if you regulate the Prana, you regulate the mind automatically. There are number of Pranayamic exercises that a teacher can help you learn. The more regulated "breath of life" or "vital breath" is, the better the result. This is further discussed in Chapter Two.

35. Vishayavati Va Pravruttir Utpanna Manasah Sthiti Nibandhini

Vishayavati=concentrated, Va=or, Pravruttir=experienced by the senses, Utpanna=brought about, Manasah=of the mind, Sthit=Steadiness, Nibandhini=cause

Or the concentration on subtle sense perceptions can cause steadiness of mind.

Dr. Rao writes, [At certain points during initial practice of concentration, various extraordinary sense perceptions can occur. They themselves could become the helpful objects for further concentration to make the mind calm and steady. If you practice Yoga and do not see any benefit, you might lose interest and begin to question its power to bring about the desired result. So to make you more confident you can concentrate on the extraordinary sense perceptions that can come after continuous practices.]

36. Vis Oka Va Jyotismati

Visoka=blissful, Va=or, Jyotismati=the supreme light

Or by concentrating on the supreme ever blissful light within.

If this is not possible one can at first imagine a brilliant white light. If this proves impossible, a candle can be used. Once the light of the candle becomes a memory, one uses the memory of that light until it becomes a reality.

37. Vita Raga Vishayam Va Chittam

Vita=free from, Raga=attachment, Vishayam=for sense objects, Va=or, Chittam=mind-composite

Or by concentrating on a great soul's mind or heart that you feel had no attachment to sense objects.

This "great soul" could be Mother Mary for Christians, Moses, Mohammad, Buddha, Krishna or anyone who you believe had a pure heart. The purpose is to dwell on something above you to find serenity.

38. Sapna Nidra Jnanalambanam Va

Svapna=dream, Nidra=deep sleep, Jnana=experience, Alambanam=to hold attention

Or by concentrating on an experience you might have had during a dream or deep sleep.

Dr. Rao writes, [Many times when we are asleep, we dream of a higher plane. To recall that dream or experience can be serene and rewarding. The peace one had during sleep can also be an experience to concentrate on to reach Samadhi. Not sleep itself but the calmness of the sleep.]

40. Paramanu Paramnma hatvantosya Vasikarah

Paramanu=primal atom, Paramamahatva=greatest magnitude, Anta=end, Asya=his, Vasikarah=mastery

Dr. Rao writes, [Gradually one's mastery in concentration extends from the primal atom to the greatest magnitude. The Yogi's mind thus by meditating becomes unobstructed from the atomic to infinity. The mind, by this practice, easily contemplates the most minute as well as the biggest things and thus the mind waves become fainter. Practice of meditation enables us to acquire unobstructed mastery from the smallest atom to inconceivable magnitude.]

When the Chitta, or mind-composite, reaches the level of complete mastery, the cosmic forces operating in the individual Chittam will expand it into cosmic Chittam, and it will attain a cosmically balanced state and power of thought transformation.

41. Kshina Vrittir Abhijathasyeva Manergrahitri Grahana Grahyesh Tatstha Tadanjanata Samapattih

Kshina=totally weakened, waned or dwindled, Vrittir=modifications
Abhijathasya=naturally pure, Iva=like, Maner=crystal, Grahitri=knower, Grahana=knowable, Grhyeshu=knowledge=Tatsha=similar, Tadanjanatha=taking the color of, Smapattih=Samadhi or balanced state

A naturally pure crystal assumes the shapes and colors of the objects near by. A Yogi's mind, with its substantially reduced modifications (Vrittis) becomes clear and balanced and attains perfection when associated with the knower, knowable and knowledge. The culmination of all meditation is Samadhi, or contemplation.

Right after World War II my uncle acquired a German Luger. While cleaning it, the pistol discharged and my aunt screamed. There had been a bullet in the chamber and it hit her in the leg. My uncle wrapped my aunt's leg in a sheet and rushed her to the doctor. After the doctors had attended to my aunt, a nurse noticed that my uncle's leg was also bleeding. It turned out that the bullet had passed through *his* leg first and then into my aunt's leg. Upon seeing his own wound my uncle immediately passed out. However, until he was made aware that he too had been shot, his mind was so involved in my Aunt's pain that he was unaware of his own.

To say a Yogi's mind has totally weakened modifications is to say that the Yogi's mind has cultivated one thought form at the cost of others. When we cultivate one thought alone, all the other impressions become weaker. Dr. Rao gives this example, [If we concentrate on the development of the mind alone, we are apt to ignore the other parts of the body. If you develop one idea through constant meditation, all other thoughts and desires will gradually fade away.] For example, if you are interested in someone, you think of that person day and night and lose interest in all other people and things. The same is true in Yoga practice. Our concentration and meditation should be as single minded as the hopelessly-in-love.

This same process is used in trying to stop a bad habit. You do not have to fight to stop a habit. Just do not give it the opportunity to repeat itself. Any kind of habit can be removed by this mental procedure. The procedure involves cultivating good and proper habits. The mind must have something to hold on to; so occupy it with good habits and all the bad habits will vanish.

The mind of a Yogi attains a state in which there is no difference between the knower, the knowable and knowledge. All three become one; either subject becomes object or object becomes subject. When there is no subject-object separation, there is no process either. The mind is completely absorbed and loses itself in the idea or the object of meditation.

Patanjali gives us the example of an object near a crystal. If we put a red flower near a crystal, it appears red like the flower. It becomes one with that, it accepts that. So too, the mind accepts the idea of your meditation and takes that form.

42. Tatra Shabdardha Jnana Vikalpaih Samkirna Savitarka

Tatra=there, Sabda=sound, word, name, Ardha=meaning, object form, Jnana=knowledge, idea, Vikalpaih=assumptions, Smakirna=mixed-up, Savitarka=deliberation

The Samadhi in which name, form and knowledge of them is mixed is called Savitarka Samadhi (with deliberation).

As any good teacher does, Patanjali tries again and with more clarity to define, in this Sutra and the following ones till the end of Chapter One, the different kinds of Samadhis. He once again reminds us of Samprajnata Samadhis, Savitarka, Savichara, Sa-ananda and Sa-asmita.

In this Sutra, he says that in Savitarka Samadhi, you can actually understand the sound, the meaning and resulting knowledge of an object. Normally, every time we hear a sound, we simultaneously do all three: hear the sound, try to understand the object denoted by the sound, and gain knowledge of the object. For example, when you hear the word "bird", the sound enters the brain and tries to find a similar groove or impression that was made when you heard it before. It has been said that every time you learn something it creates a new wrinkle on the surface of your brain. Today people burn disks when they wish to record sounds. Years ago the same sounds were recorded on the grooves on LP records. Similarly, our brains create memory grooves to record impressions. Because you hear the word "bird", and it is you have heard it before, a connection is made. So the word, the object and the knowledge, Sabda, Artha and Jnana, happen simultaneously, but in this Samadhi we can separate them one after another and we can arrest the process when and where we want.

43. Smruti Parishudhau Svarupa Sunya Iva Artha Matra Nirbhasa Nirvitarka

Smruti=memory, Parisudhau=well purified, Svarupa=its own nature, Sunya=empty, Iva=as it were, Arhta=object, form, only, Nirbhasa=shining, Nirvitarka=without deliberation

When the memory is well purified, the knowledge of the object of concentration shines alone, devoid, of the distinction of name and quality. This is Nirvitarka Samadhi, without deliberation.

When the memory is purified or devoid of any particular power of property, then there is only the knowledge of the object meditated upon ignoring the sound and object. Ignoring the sound and object, Sabda and Artha, you gain the knowledge (Jnana) alone.

44. Etayaiva Savichara Nirvichara Cha Sukshama Vishaya Vyakhyata

Etaya=in the same way, Eva=only, Savichara=reflective, Nirvichara=super (or non=reflective), Cha=and, Sukshama=subtle, Vishaya=objects, Vyakhyata=are explained

In the same way, Savichara (reflective) and Nirvichara (Super or non-reflective) Samadhis, which are practiced upon subtle objects, are explained.

45. Suhshma Vishayatvam Chalinga Paryavasnam

Suhsama=subtle, Vishayatvam=objectiveness, Cha=and, Alinga=indefinable, Paryavasanam=end only at

The subtlety of possible objects of concentration ends only at the indefinable.

The objects, mind-composite and ego ultimately end in the primal force called the Prakruti ("the primordial basic substance") in its un-manifested condition. In that condition there is no name, no form and no thought, only the fully balanced, tranquil un-manifested state of nature (the universe). So the mind has the power to go to the very root of the un-manifested nature.

46. Tha Eva Sabijah Samadhih

Tha=they, Eva=all, Sabihjah with seed, Samadhih=contemplation

All these Samadhis are Sabihjah with seed which could bring one back
into bondage or mental disturbance.

These contemplations do not destroy the seeds of past actions, and thus cannot give liberation. The previously mentioned four states of thought transformation are called seeded Samadhis because in all of them, the less than pure tendencies are not completely destroyed. Their growth is just arrested and remain in the form of Beeja (seed), in the subconscious state of mind-composite. According to time, space, cause and effect, they can be germinated again if the student/Yogi is careless in his/her self-discipline. Unless the seeds are also destroyed weeds will reappear every spring even if the plant is uprooted.

47. Nirvichara Vaisharadhye Adhyatma Prasadah

Nirvichara=non-reflective, Vaisharadhye=pure, Adhyatma=pure
Self, Prasadah=shines

In the pure state of Nirvichara Samadhi, the Supreme Self shines.

In the pure state of Nirvichara Samadhi the mind-composite becomes firmly fixed. At that point, the undisturbed flow of the ultra-meditative state causes subjective luminosity of Spiritual Light. When the student/Yogi has achieved union with the Light of the Supreme, Purusha, he/she is no longer at the mercy of the law of action, Karma and fate. He/She, has reached the "high tower" of meditation and looks upon all fellow beings with great love and compassion.

48. Ritambhara Tatra Prajana

Ritambhara=absolute true, Tatra=this is, Prajna=consciousness

This is Ritambhara Prajna or the absolute true consciousness. After attaining the pure non-reflective Samadhi, the Yogi gets "wisdom-filled-with-truth." What is this actually? Patanjali says:

49. Sruthanumana Prajnyabhyam Anyavishaya Visesharthatvat

Srutha=(heard) study of scriptures, Anum=inference, Prajnybyam=
from the knowledge, Any=totally different, Vishaya Visesha=special truth, Ardhatvat=cognition of

Dr. Rao writes, [This special truth is totally different from knowledge gained by hearing, study of scripture or inference. When Ritambhara Prajna is achieved we understand everything without study. When we transcend the mind through proper concentration, we feel the cosmic force or God. You can check your experience with the scriptures or through the word of saints and sages, but it is known by you through your own experience. Until then, all you have heard and read and visualized will be by your own mind. Experiencing God is something that is genuine and comes only when you transcend the mind. God cannot be understood by the mind because mind is matter, and matter cannot possibly understand something more subtle than matter. So in Ritambhara Prajna you transcend the mind and gain knowledge that is realization. For that the mind must be completely silent.]

50. Tajjah Samskaronya Samskarah Prathibandhi

Tajjah=there from, Samskarah=impression, Anya=other, Samskara=impressions, Prathibandhi=wipes out

The impression (memory or Samskara) produced by this Samadhi wipes out all the other impressions (memories).

The impression that results from this Samadhi (by which you get Ritambhara Prajna) will ultimately obstruct all other impressions (memories or Samskaras). Everything dies away and you will no longer be an ordinary person, ignorant of his/her true nature. When you reach this stage you will never lose this knowledge. In this stage you become a Jivanmukta, a realized saint. Jivan means "one who lives" and Mukta means "liberated", so such a person is a liberated being. You live, eat, and talk like anybody else, even do business like anybody else, but still you are liberated. A Jivanmukta may do anything. He does not need to be in a cave or on a mountaintop contemplating his navel; they may be anywhere. A Jivanmukta may be involved in the world for the sake of humanity without any personal attachment. Prompted by the Higher Will; he does what he can and passes through the world virtually unnoticed. He will not be attached to anything. In this state no impressions and no old thoughts will bring him back into ordinary life. Although he appears to be normal, the seeds of all mental impressions are completely burnt out, and thus he always lives in that unattached state.

51. Tasyapi Nirodhe Sarvanitradhan Niribihah samadhih

Tasyapi=even this, Nirodhe=wiped out, Sarva=Nirbijah=seedless, Samadhih=samadhi

Dr. Rao writes, [Now Patanjali describes the highest Samadhi. Even with Ritambhara Prajna the subtle mind is there. There is still a division between the Prajna, or wisdom, and the owner of that wisdom. Even the feeling of having realized God, should go. Then you are completely free. You have attained Nirbija Samadhi. There is no more birth or death for you; you realize your immortality. It leaves nothing and the Soul is manifested as It is, in its own glory. Then alone we realize that the Soul is not a compound but it is one without a second and that is only eternal, simple in the universe, such as it cannot be born, cannot die, It is immortal, indestructible, the ever living essence of intelligence,Sat Chit Ananda.]

Dr. V.S. Rao's comments were adapted from those of: H.R. Swami Vivekananda, H.R. Swami Sivananda Saraswata, H.R. Swami Saraswati, H.R. Swami Brahmananda Sarswati, and H.H. Yogeswar Rama La Ji Maharaj.

# INTRODUCTION TO CHAPTER TWO

▼

At the end of Chapter One, I provided a list of men from whom Dr. Rao adapted many of his comments on the Sutras. Dr. Rao used these comments to explain Yoga to me. Please note that much of Yogic thought is derived from the interpretation of Yogic writing by as many as four distinct lineages of Yoga Masters that date back over two millennia. So when I write "Patanjali says" or "Patanjali means," these thoughts are attributed to him, but likely adapted from other Yogis.

Some of these learned men's commentaries may differ because they attended different universities and/or belonged to different associations where Yogic thought has been examined, re-examined and taught. The differences arise from interpretation, so Dr. Rao focuses on his interpretation just as different denominations of Protestants or Catholics focus on different aspects of the words spoken by Jesus over two thousand years ago.

When the apostle John wrote the "Book of Revelations," a prophetic vision of the end of the world in the New Testament of the Bible, he was in a jail cell on the Greek island of Pathos. If I am not mistaken, his jailors were Roman, and it is highly possible that they were illiterate. If they had been literate they would not have been assigned such a menial task. To protect himself, just in case the Romans were literate, John wrote his letters in a very low dialect of Greek called Koine. John's writings were not translated into Hebrew. St. Jerome later translated them from Koine into Latin and from Latin they were translated into every language on earth including my own, English. Anyone who has ever told something to another person, who in turn has told it to someone else, knows that the final thought usually ends up slightly different from the original. What is read in English today may not be exactly the vision that was revealed to John in his jail cell. However, I do not want to debate my theory. The point I am trying to make is that when you see the words "Patanjali means" or "Patanjali says" in this commentary or others of the Yoga Sutras, they tend to be opinions passed down from Guru to Guru verbally and in writing for over four dozen generations. There will be many interpretations of Patanjali's Sutras and because of their cryptic nature it may take a commentator two hundred words to explain five of Patanjali's words to the casual observer. Yet some are so simple that the translation speaks for itself, just like when Christ said, "Do unto others as you would have them do unto you."

Having said that, Patanjali in Chapter One stated that Samadhi, (contemplation or Super Consciousness), could be obtained by those whose mind-composite is pure and clear. Very few people have attained that level of mind-composite. So here in Chapter Two he describes the means by which to attain a concentrated state of mind, for those whose minds are restless and distracted—which is almost everyone. Naturally, the mind is congested with various impurities that may have come from innumerable births or even just events in the present life and cannot be removed without self-discipline and purification. In Chapter Two Patanjali's Sutras will explain more about such self-discipline and purification.

A casual observer or reader should know that at this point a Yoga student has finished with his internal debate and is satisfied. He now only studies to intensify and reinforce his convictions. As I pointed out earlier, he realizes that knowledge is infinite and time is short. So take the essence of knowledge and leave the dross. In short, what is contained in Chapter Two may be of some help to you, but to some it may not. This book is about suggestions, not commandments. Please do not skip from Chapter One to Chapter Three just to find out how to walk on water; I want to help you not drown you.

Sri Sankara says, [Do not argue, do not answer any argument, but calmly go away since arguments only disturb the mind. You have to train the intellect but do not disturb it for nothing, such as futile argumentation. You have to go beyond intellect, which is limited by the senses. Every argument throws the mind into confusion, which is a drawback. So be silent and do not argue. Surrendering the fruits of your work to God is not taking credit or blame to ourselves, but to give up both to God and be at peace.]

Patanjali says that the Samadhis are very difficult to attain and must be taken up slowly. The first step is called "Kriya", which is the process of working towards Yoga.

I want to reiterate that most of these thoughts and commentaries are compilations, and I have modified them when I felt it necessary to better explain Yoga to you.

# YOGA DARSAN OF PATANJALI

## CHAPTER 2

▼

# SADHANA PADA—ON PRACTICE

1. Tapah Svadhya Isvara Pranidhanani Kriya Yogah

Tapah=self-discipline, Svadhaya=study of spiritual books, Isvara =Supreme Being, Pranidhanani=surrendering, Kriya Yogah=Yoga in practice

Self-discipline for purification, study of spiritual books and surrender to the Supreme Being constitute Yoga in practice.

Tapas has been defined as "a means to burn or create heat." Anything burned out will be purified, like gold for instance. This process also relates to mental impurities. It is by accepting all the pain that comes to us, even though the nature of the mind is to chase after pleasure. We can accept mental pain if we keep in mind its purifying effects. Such acceptance makes the mind steady and strong because it ensures endurance and self-discipline. Such discipline obviously cannot be practiced in meditation rooms, only in our daily lives as we relate to other people.

Many Yoga practitioners believe that this Sutra means to hold a posture (asana) past the point of pain at or near the point when injury occurs. Yoga is about self-discipline not self-torture. In the method called "Upasya", people practice all sorts of self-torture. Some ascetics lie on beds of nails or keep one arm raised in the air so that the arm gets thinner and thinner until it finally decays. Lord Krishna said, "These persons are demons because they disturb the pure Self who dwells within their bodies." So self-torture is not self-discipline. Self-discipline is an aid to spiritual progress, whereas torture is an obstacle.

Lord Krishna divides true austerities into three groups: physical, verbal and mental. He classifies worship, purity, straightforwardness, celibacy and non-injury as the austerities of the body. Austerity of speech should bring tranquility, and be truthful, pleasant and beneficial. The Upanishad verse "Satyam Bruyat, Priyam Bruyat" means "speak what is true, speak what is pleasant." Sri Krishna describes serenity of mind, good-heartedness, self-control and purity of nature as the mental austerities.

Svadyaya, or study, concerns the true Self. Anything that will elevate the mind and remind you of your true Self should be studied, such as the *Bhagavad-Gita*, *Bible*, *Koran* or any uplifting scripture. Many Yoga teachers believe that they must teach their students Hinduism or to chant in Sanskrit. This however, is an erroneous interpretation of this Sutra. Yoga teachers should be sensitive to each student's religious beliefs and not impose their beliefs on their students.

The last part of Kriya Yoga is surrendering to the Supreme Being. Dedicate the fruits of actions to God. Dedicate everything, your Japa (mantra repetition), your practice, to the Lord. Sri Paramesvararpanamastu. If you remember to do this constantly, the mind will be free and tranquil. Dedication is true Yoga! Say, "I am yours". "All is yours". "Your will be done". Remember "mine" binds and "yours" liberates. So change all instances of "mines" into "yours" and you will be happy always.

2. Samadhi Bhavanarthah Klesha Tanukaranarthatcha

Samadhi=contemplation, Bhavanarthath=to get into, Klesha=obstacles, Tanukaranarthta=minimize, Cha=and

The practice of Kriya Yoga will minimize the obstacles that prevent you from achieving Samadhi. Without Kriya Yoga you can never overcome your obstacles and reach Samadhi. Everything you do in Hatha yoga, Japa Yoga, and studying with a Yoga teacher is preparation for meditation and Samadhi, (contemplation).

3. Avidha Asmita Raga Dvesha Abhiniveshah Kleshah

Avidya=ignorance, Asmita=egoism, Raga=attachment, Dvesha=hatred, Abhinivesha=clinging to bodily life, Kleshah=obstacles

Ignorance, egoism, attachment, hatred and clinging to bodily life are the five obstacles.

In the previous Sutra Patanjali names the five obstacles (kleshas) that stand in the way to achieving bliss and explains them in the following Sutras. The order is significant. Because of the ignorance of Self, the ego begins to dominate. Due to this enlarged ego there is attachment to things for selfish pleasure. We become attached to things we have and to things we want, and losing them, or even not getting them is upsetting. Finally, as we are attached to things and afraid of our death, we cling to life in the body. All mental afflictions are pain-bearing obstacles (kleshas). They manifest in forms of Avidya (ignorance or unreal cognition), which is the result of incorrect perception, illusion and misinterpretation and leads one to a lower nature, bringing new afflictions and allowing the vicious circle to stay in motion. These are the five pains that bind us. Ignorance is the cause, and the other four are its effects.

4. Avidya Kshetram Uttaresham Prasupta Tanu Vicchinna Udaranam

Avidya=ignorance, Kshetram=field, Uttaresham=for the others mentioned after it, Prasupta=whether they are dormant, Tanu=feeble Vicchinna=intercepted, Udaranam=or sustained

Ignorance is the field for the others mentioned after it, whether they are dormant, feeble, intercepted or sustained.

Patanjali says that Kleshas, afflictions that may be dormant, feeble, intercepted, or sustained in the mind-composite, have their existence in ignorance, and ignorance is the productive field. A baby's obstacles are completely dormant, and the baby seems to be innocent. But, as the baby matures, the inborn disposition will emerge and the baby will not remain innocent. Ignorance and the obstacles that lay dormant in the mind will surface at the proper time. The second affliction is in the mind of an advanced Yoga practitioner whose afflictions are feeble but not completely free of the Kleshas (obstacles). They are at the bottom of the mind-lake in a very subtle form and out of disuse become weak. The third state of intercepted development is seen in the mind of a beginning practitioner. Here, the obstacles are temporarily pushed down by constant practice of virtuous qualities such as love, truthfulness, cheerfulness, kindness, discipline etc. If such a seeker is not careful to cultivate these virtues, even for a few days, the obstacles will immediately come to the surface. In the case of an average person, the fourth affliction is seen. Since the Kleshas constantly manifest, and since obstructions affect the average persons mind constantly, he will have no say over them because he lacks the tools to exert any force to control them.

5. Anitya Asuchi Duhka Anatmasu Nitya Suchi Sukha Atma Khyatir Avidya

Anitya=impermanent, Asuchi=impure, Duhka=painful, Anatma=non-self, Nitya=permanent, Suchi=pure, Sukha=pleasant, Khyatir=cognition, Avidya=ignorance

Ignorance is regarding the impermanent as permanent, the impure as pure, the painful as pleasant and the non-self as self.

Dr. Rao writes, ["What is Self and what is non-self? The Self is the eternal, never-changing One. It is always everywhere as the very basic substance. All things are actually only the Self, but in our ignorance we see them as different objects. Thus we take changing appearances to be the unchanging truth. When something changes, it cannot be the Self. For instance, our own bodies are changing every minute. Yet we take the body to be our Self. We say "I am hungry," "I am white," "I am lame." These are all just conditions and qualities of the body. We touch the truth when we say, "my body is cold," "my mind is calm," implying that the body and mind belong to us and that therefore we are not the body nor the mind, they are just ours. The body, which is a vehicle for enjoyment, and the mind, which is a vehicle for the True Self that is God, are manifestations of non-self. The idea that any of them or all them are Self, is called Avidya, or ignorance.]

6. Drig Darsana Saktyor Edatamata Iva Asmita

Drig=seer, Darsana=instrument of seeing, Saktyor=powers, Edatamata =identify, Iva=as it were, Asmita=Egoism

Egoism is the identification, as it were, of the power of the seer, Purusha, with that of the instrument of seeing, namely, body-mind.

In this Sutra, Patanjali explains egoism. The ego is the reflection of the true Self on the mind. The two appear to be same, but one is the original, the other is a reflected duplicate. The Self will always be misrepresented by the ego until our ignorance is removed. Purusha (true Self which is God) is the subjective power of

Consciousness, and Chitta (mind-composite) is the objective instrumental power of seeing and feeling. The appearance of these two powers, although they are identical is the affliction known as Asmita, or egoism.

7. Suhhanusayi Ragah

Sukha=pleasure, Anusayi=follows with, Ragah=attachment

Attachment is that which follows identification with pleasurable experiences.

8. Duhkhananusayi Dveshah

Duhkha=pain, Anusayi=followed with, Dvesha=aversion
Aversion is that which follows identification with painful experience.

Dr. Rao writes, [Attachment to pleasure, or Raga, is another pain-bearing obstacle. We attach ourselves to pleasure because we expect happiness from it, forgetting that happiness is always in us as the true Self. When we expect joy from outside things we become attached to those things. If we find these things make us unhappy, we create an aversion, or Dvesha, towards them. So Raga and Dvesha, likes and dislikes, are impediments in the spiritual path. One we like because it seems to bring happiness, the other we dislike because it seems to bring us unhappiness.]

9. Svarasavati Vidushipi Tatha Rudhobhinesah

Savrasa=by its own potency, Vati=flowing, Vidushipi=due to past experience, Rudhobehinesah=exists even in the wise

The next obstacle is Abhinivesa, "clinging to life ". Yoga reminds us that all our knowledge comes through experience. Without experience, we cannot understand or learn anything. Even books remind us of something we have experienced in the past, which was buried in the mind-composite and was waiting to resurface. The words of others sometimes help kindle a fire that is already in us. The fire must be there first, for the kindling stick to ignite it. If you have never tasted an *anona* fruit from Costa Rica, I could explain it to you for hours, but you could not experience the taste I tried to convey. Instinct is a trace of experience that has been repeated to the point that the impressions have sunk down to the bottom of the mental lake. They arise when the atmosphere is created to allow it to surface. All experiences are stored in the mind-composite. Patajanli believed that is why we fear death. Through reincarnation we have died a hundred times before, and the pangs of those moments color our souls. The moment we get a new body, we become afraid to leave it; we create a sentimental attachment to it and cling to it. We even kill other human beings if it is necessary in order to protect ourselves and to remain in our bodies as long as possible.

10. Te Pratiprasava Heyah Suhshmah

Te=these, Pratiprasave=resolving back to their cause, Heyah=destroyed, Suhshmah=subtle

In subtle form, these obstacles can be destroyed by resolving them back into their primal cause, the ego.

11. Dhyana Heyah Tad Vrittayah

Dhyana=by meditation, Heyah=destroyed, Tad=their, Vrittayah=active modifications

Dr. Rao said that hindering thoughts come in two stages: the potential form, before they come to the surface and are converted to action, and the manifesting ones, which are put into action. Thoughts form in a potential state. Samskaras cannot be removed by meditation. On the contrary, when you meditate on these impressions, they rise back to the surface. You cannot destroy them by these means but you can see and understand them well enough to control whether or not they should be allowed to manifest into action. You can trace them back into their subtle form and see directly that the ego is the basis for all these obstructing thoughts. Then, when you transcend the mind in the higher Samadhi, even the ego is lost. When you let go of the ego, all the impressions in it will also be lost. Until that occurs, however, the impressions will remain.

12. Klesamulah Karmasayo Drihtadrushata Janma Vidaniyam

Klesa=obstacles, Mulah=the root, Karmashayah=reservoir or the womb of the Karmas, Krishta=seen or present, Adrishta=unseen or future, Janma=birth, Vidaniyam=experienced

The womb of Karmas, actions and reaction, has its roots in these obstacles, and the Karmas being experienced in the seen (present) or in the unseen (future) births.

In this Sutra Patanjali tries to explain what Karma is, how it is stored and how it functions. Karma has been defined as "action and/or the results of action". Every action we perform is accompanied by a reaction. A popular phrase states, "Whatever you do will come back on you." This is the general definition of Karma—

present reactions to past actions. Every action will leave its result and every cause will bear its effect. What came first, the chicken or the egg? The seed before the plant? Likewise, it is impossible to know the origin of Karma. No one knows when, where and how it started. So, after your action, what happens? Patanjali says the action is stored in a theoretical receptacle for the Karmas called the Karmashaya, or "the womb of Karmas". Theoretically, the Karmas wait for an opportunity to come to the surface and bring their reaction. Patanjali believed the Kleshas (obstacles) cause these Karmas. Once an obstacle has manifested, an action has to be taken. The result of the action—the reaction—may bear fruit now or in a future birth. According to the number of our Karmas, we will have more births. There need not be a separate birth for every Karma; they may group together. One strong Karma may call for a body, and all other similar Karmas that can make use of that particular vehicle to bring their reaction will join in. When that Karma is over, there will be many more waiting in line.

Of course, this is all theoretical. Another theory, held by many Roman Catholics, suggests that there is a storage area for the soul called Purgatory. Purgatory is the state of purification through suffering after death from venial (capable of being forgiven) sins committed in this life. Why would a soul be in Purgatory? The general wisdom is that the vehicle for the soul accomplished to few good actions (good Karmas), or conversely, committed too many bad actions—to allow it to go forth from the past life. I hope you can see the similarities to the Karmashaya here. Where were the "good deeds" needed to pass through a state similar to purgatory stored? Patanjali called it the Karmashaya, or womb of the Karmas.

Patanjali says there are three kinds of Karmas: those being expressed and exhausted through this birth (Prarabdha Karma); new Karmas being created during this birth (Agami Karma); and those waiting in the Karmashaya to be fulfilled in future births (Sanjita Karma). Imagine a bowman who has a quiver of arrows, and the quiver being the Karmashaya. A really expert bowman can shoot one arrow, and before it lands, he will have another arrow fitted in the bow. The arrows would be in different stages of flight. The first arrow is the Prarabdha Karma; it has left the bow and cannot be retrieved. As long as the body stays here, it will indirectly or directly be affected by what you have already done in the past. Also, as long as the body stays here it will continue to be supplied by more arrows that were allocated to it. The second arrow (Agami Karma) is the Karma you create now and have control over. The arrows in the quiver (Karmashaya) can either stay there or be shot. We control the Agami directly and the Sanjita indirectly, but we cannot do anything about the Pralabdha; we must simply accept it. Yogis believe that this will continue until Self-Realization.

13. Sati Mule Tad Vipako Jatyayur Bhogah

Sati=with the existence, Mule=of the root, Tad=its, Vipaka=fruits, Jati=birth of a species of life, Ayuh=their span, Bhogah=experiences

With the existence of the root, there will be fruits also, namely, the births of different species of life, their life spans and experiences.

Dr. Rao says we should think about what species we may belong to in our next birth. We need not get a human body. If our thoughts are animalistic, the Karmas may give us an animal's body. If someone is cunning in this life, the reactions will bring forth more cunning actions that might be better expressed through a fox's body. This does not contradict the theory of evolution. The individual soul always continues to evolve, even though the individual may receive various bodies that are evolved to a greater or lesser degree: the soul itself experiences things constantly through these different bodily forms, however, and so it continues to progress. Remember, the body is not the experienced entity. Life is experienced by the mind through the body. It is the mind that experiences and enjoys everything, not the organs of the body.

Even in an animal's body, the mind experiences and undergoes things. When we gain experience, we progress, we purge our past Karmas until we eventually reach our destination.

In our journey towards Self-realization, each body is a different vehicle. A deer in the forest may have once been a saint who, by a small mistake, received that body. Thus we cannot say they are mere animals. Within each form lies a soul on its evolutionary path towards Self-realization. The Sutra also says that the span of each life (Ayu) and experience of pleasure or pain, (Bhoga) are determined by Karma, which in turn is the fruit of all the obstacles mentioned before.

14. Te Hlada Paritapa Phalah Punyapunya Hetutvat

Te=they, Hlada=pleasure, Paritapa=pain, Phalah=fruits, Punya=merit, Apunya=demerit, Hdtutvat=cause

The Karmas bear fruits of pleasure and pain caused by merit or demerit.

Dr. Rao teaches that if you have done something meritorious, you experience pleasure and happiness, but if you have been wrong, then you will suffer. A happy or unhappy life is our own creation.

15. Parinama Tapa Samskara Kuhkhair Guna Vritti Virodhacca Duhkam Eva Sarvam Vivekinam

Parimama=consequence, Tapa=anxiety, Samskara=impression, Kuhkhair=pain, Guna=qualities, Vritti=functioning, Vritti=functioning modifications, Virodhat=contradiction, Cha=and, Duhkam=painful, Eva=indeed, Sarvam=all, Vivekinam=to the person of discrimination

To one of discrimination, everything is painful indeed, due to its consequences. The anxiety and fear over losing what is gained, the resulting impressions left in the mind to create renewed cravings and the constant conflict among the three gunas (constituents of nature), which can temporarily control the mind.

This is an important Sutra and a great spiritual truth. All experiences are painful for a person of spiritual discrimination. In this world, all experiences that come from outside through the world, through nature or material things, are ultimately painful. None can give everlasting happiness. They may give temporary pleasure but they always end in pain. Even the enjoyment of our present pleasure is usually painful because we fear its loss.

Dr. Rao says that wherever we are, we have to learn to handle things properly. We cannot always be changing environments, running here and there. But once we know how to handle one small family, we can handle a larger group. If you cannot face a sharp word from your beloved, how can you face such words from a stranger? The world is a training place where we learn to use the gifts of this life without getting attached. Instead of saying, "to one of discrimination, everything is painful", think "to one of discrimination everything is pleasurable." A person with such an understanding has the magic wand to convert everything into happiness. Pleasure and pain are but the outcome of our approach. By detaching ourselves completely from the entire world and standing aloof from it, we can choose to live in heaven or hell.

16. Heyam Kuhkam Anagatam

Heyam=avoidable, Kuhkam=pain, Anagatam=not yet come

Pain that has not yet come is avoidable.

Dr. Rao teaches that past pain and present pain do not fall in the list of the avoidable. When pain has passed, or is in progress, it can be reduced by medicine and meditation. Pain that has not yet come is most troublesome, since it is present in the subconscious state of the mind-composite Chitta, and has not yet sprouted from its seed form. Hence it can be rooted out by meditation. Pain in progress is relatively insignificant but the possibility of future pain is mighty and far reaching. If this pain is not uprooted it will cause suffering. However, one can use meditation to avoid this suffering.

Avoid dwelling on the future during meditation, as it causes anxiety and disturbs the mind-composite.

> 17. Drashtri Drisyayoh Samyoga Heya Hetuh
>
> Drashtri=the seer, Drisyayoh=the seen, Samyogah=union, Heya=avoidable, Hetuh=cause
>
> The cause of that avoidable pain is the union of the seer (purusha) and the seen (prakruti or Nature).

Patanjali asserts that the cause of pain is the union of the seer and the seen. Yoga philosophy speaks of two important things; one is the Purusha (true self, which is God or the Seer), and the other is the Prakruti. Dr. Rao says that the Purusha is the true self and it is the one that sees. The Prakruti is everything else. All things besides you are the seen. But it seems that we always identify ourselves with the seen, with what we possess. As the Self, all things are possessed by us. That is why we say, "my body, my mind, my knowledge." Everything we call ours cannot be us. We speak of ourselves in two ways. One example is, "Look at my body. Is it not slim?" Are you speaking of you here or your body? This identification with other things is the cause of all our pain. Instead, if we are always just ourselves, things may change or stay as they are, but they will never cause us pain. Patanjali says stay in your own true Self. If you do this, you will always be happy with your true Self.

> 18. Prakaas Kriya Sthiti Silam Bhutendriyatmakam Bhogapavargarthadrisyam Bhogapavargartha drisyam
>
> Prakasda=illumination, Kriya=activity, Sthiti=inertia, Silam=nature, Bhuta=elements, Indriya=inertia, Silam=nature, Indriya=sense organs, Atmakam=consists of, Bhoga=experience, Apavarga=liberation, Artham=its purpose, Drisyam=the seen

The seen is of the nature of the gunas—illumination, activity and inertia—and consists of the elements and sense organs whose purpose is to provide both experiences and liberation for the Purusha.

In this statement, Patanjali talks about the "drisya", or seen. "Atma" or Pursha or the seer that all denote the same entity, the true you. You become a knower because there is a known. You become a seer because there is something to see. Here, Patanjali tries to analyze what this "seen" is that gives us experience. He says it is a combination of different elements and organs controlled by the three gunas. He uses the term's "prakasa kriya sthiti". Prakasa means "illumination" and stands for "sattva" (tranquility). "Kriya" is "action" and represents rajas. "Sthiti" is "inertia", or tamas. Dr. Rao writes, [Why does Prakriti (nature) exist? Nature is here to give you experience and ultimately to liberate you from its bondage. Even if people do not want to be liberated, it educates them gradually so that one day they will come to feel, "I'm tired of the whole thing. I don't want it anymore. I've had enough." When will we feel this way? Only after we've gotten enough kicks and burns. The purpose of Prakriti is to give you those knocks. So, we should never condemn nature.]

19. Visesavisea lingamatralingani guna parvani.

Visesha=specific, avisesha=non-specific, lingamatra=defined, alingani=indefinable, guna=qualities, parvani=stages.

The stages of the gunas are specific, non-specific, defined and indefinable.

Here, Patanjali analyzes Prakriti with more clarity. He divides all of nature into four stages going in reverse order from the way he expresses them. First there is the un-manifested, or avyakta, the stage in which nature is static or indefinable. A slightly more manifested stage is defined next. The third is a more developed stage where nature forms into the subtle senses, buddhi (intellect) and the mind. And the fourth stage is the gross objects, which we can hear, feel, see, touch, smell and taste.

We normally only understand things we can see. However, if we develop a subtler perception, we can also see subtler things. For instance, we can see a flower itself but we can only sense its smell—we cannot see it. Even the smell is matter, although it is very subtle; if we have developed a enough perception, we can subtle perception we can see it emanating from the blossom like a magnetic field. Although each individual has as an aura, or color, we normally see bodies and not their auras. However, we can develop over time the subtle senses needed to see them.

20. Drasta Drismatrah Suddhopi Pratyayanupasyah

Drashta=the Seer, drismatrah=the power of seeing, suddhopi=although pure, pratayaya=through the mind, anupasyah=appears as if seeing

The Seer is nothing but the power of seeing which, although pure, appears to see through the mind.

After discussing Prakriti, Patanjali talks about the Seer, or Purusha. Even though light is pure and constant, it appears to change because of the medium of nature. The sun's rays appear to bend when they pass through a section of water, although they do not actually bend. A filament gives pure white light but appears red because of the red glass that surrounds it. Likewise, we are all of the same light, but we do not look alike because of the nature of our bodies and minds.

21. Tandarhtha Eva Drushasyatam

Tandarhtaha=for His (the Purushas) sake, Eva=only, Drisyasya=the seen (Prakruti) Atma=exists

The seen exists only for the sake of the seer.

Patanjali explained in the previous Sutras that nature exists to give experience to the Purusha (true self which is God), and so we think the Purusha is doing the experiencing. In reality, the Purusha is not experiencing anything. Like God it is just a witness; but does not directly intervene in wars or famine. How would we learn if not from our own mistakes? When we realize that the Purusha is neither the doer nor the enjoyer, we will change our vision and attitude, but for now, we need to start from where we are. Dr. Rao says that the very word understanding is a combination of two words, under and stand. To understand, we should stand under. But stand under what? Under where we now stand. We should know where we stand first and then try to *"understand"*, to go a little deeper. When we try to understand, we will find we are not all on one "stand" but at different levels, with different capacities, tastes and temperaments.

Each individual has his or her own stand. Someone else's understanding of anything is completely different from yours. The same scripture reads differently to different people as each one tries to interpret it for him or herself. Here Patanjali is saying we are now under the impression that the true Self is experiencing something, but one day we will know that the Self never does anything nor will it ever enjoy anything.

Nature is also called Maya, or illusion. To a person who has truly understood real nature, it is Maya (illusion) to them. To others it is still real. Dr. Rao says that the entire world is a sort of factory. In a factory, raw materials come in, pass through different processes, and emerge as finished products, which go to the showroom, the sales section; and finally to the consumer. These products do not come again to the workshop, but the workshop continues to function as raw materials keep passing through it. So too, as we pass through the world, are we not shaped every second of the way by different experiences? We become refined as our knowledge develops. Eventually, we understand the world completely and have no business being in the factory any longer. We have realized that what we thought was real—money, fame, beauty—is fleeting. The rich become poor and the beautiful become wrinkled.

22. Kritatham Pratiapi Anahtam tat Sadharanatvat

Kritatham=who has attained liberation, prati=to him, nashtam=destroyed, api=even though, anashtam=not destroyed, tat=to the, anya=others, sadharanatvat=common

Although destroyed for him who has attained liberation, it (the seen) still exists for others, being common to them.

The existence of the illusion of Self is still held and believed by those that have not reached Self-realization.

23. Sva Svamisktyoh Svarupe upalabdhi hetuh samyogha

Sva=being owned (prakriti), Svami=the Owner (Purusha), sktyoh=of their powers, svarupa=the nature, upalabdhi=recognition, hetuh=cause, samyogha=union

The union of owner (Purusha) and owned (Prakriti) causes the recognition of the nature and powers them both.

Dr. Rao says that Samyoga (union) is necessary for the Purusha to realize itself with the help of nature. Samyoga means "perfect union or junction". And here it does not mean the union of the individual self with the higher Self, but the union of the Purusha and Prakriti, Self and Nature. When they are completely apart, they do not express themselves. Their connection, however, lets us know them both. They help each other. It is something like the following: if you want to print with white letters, you must have a black background for contrast. You cannot write white letters on a white background. Through the Prakriti, we realize that we are the Purusha. If not for the Prakriti, we realize we are the Purusha. If it were not for the Prakriti, we would not know ourselves. So Prakriti is not just bondage, as many people think; it is necessary.

24. Taya Hetur Avidya

Taya=its, hetur=cause, avidya=ignorance

The cause of this union is ignorance.

25. Tad Abhavat Samyogabhavo Hanam Tat Driseh Kaivalyam.

Tad=its (ignorance), Abhavat=absence, Samyo=gabhavo Hanam Tat=that, driseh=of the Seer, Kaivalyam=independence

Without this ignorance, no such union occurs. This is the independence of the Seer.

Put more simply, once the junction created by ignorance is removed, the Seer rests in his own true nature. The Purusha (true Self) is always like that, although it temporarily appears to be bound by Prakriti (the material of Nature). We should remember this point in all our experiences, all our actions, and all our ups and downs. Ask yourself, "Did this situation harm me? Who is happy? Who is unhappy?" If we continually ask these questions and do this kind of meditation, we will find that we are only the knower. We know that many different things happen, but there is really no difference in the knowing.

The Vedantins say, "Aham sakshihi," ("I am the eternal witness"). When we are worried over a loss, we should ask, "Who is worried? Who knows I am worried?" If we conclude that the Infinite Supreme Soul knows all our worries, the worry will go away. When we analyze the worry it becomes an object, something with which we are no longer involved.

26. Vivkakhatir Aviplava Hanopayah

Vivekakhayatih=discriminative discernment, Aviplava=uninterrupted, hana=removal upayah=method

Uninterrupted discriminative discernment is the method for its removal.

Yogic Science teaches that the entire world has two aspects, permanent and impermanent, or the never-changing and the ever-changing. The essence of everything is the same, but it appears in many forms and names. On the level of form, you are not the same person now as you were last week. Even a minute ago, you were different. Every minute, the body is changing; some part is dying, and some part is being born. According to the Yogic system, the entire body changes in a period of twelve years. In other words, not have one cell that was there twelve years ago. Discrimination does not mean for instance to discriminate between what is salt and what is sugar. That is just ordinary understanding. The real discrimination is to tell the original basic *Truth*, if we did so we would never face disappointment or get upset over the changes in the forms and names. Our minds would remain steady. It is for this understanding that we say the prayer, "Lead us from the unreal to real, from darkness to light, from death to immortality." What is it that dies? A log of wood dies to become a few planks. The planks die to become a chair. The chair dies to become a piece of firewood, and the firewood dies to become ash. You give different names to the different shapes the wood takes, but the basic substance is there always.

27. Tasya Saptadha Prantabhumih Prajana

Tashaya=his, saptadha=sevenfold, prantabhumih=in the final stage, prajna=wisdom

One's wisdom in the final stage is sevenfold:

1. desire to know anything more
2. desire to stay away from anything
3. desire to gain anything new
4. desire to do anything
5. sorrow
6. fear
7. delusion

28. Yoganganusthatnad asuddhi Ksayejnanadiptir a vivekakhyateh

Yoga=union, anga=limbs, anushtanat=by the practice, assuddhi=impurity, kshaye=destruction or dwindling, jnadipthi=light of wisdom, asuddhi=leads to, vivekakhyateh=discriminative discernment

In the rest of this chapter, Patanjali gives us different ideas about Yoga practice. He divides the practice into eight stages; or limbs. That is why these Sutras are also called Ashtanga Yoga, or the eight-limbed Yoga. He elaborates over some of the same ideas he has heretofore explained up to now, but in a more practical way.

29. Yama Niyamasana Pranayama Pratyahara Dharana Dhyana Samadhayo

Yama=abstinence, niyama=observance, asana=posture, pranayama=breath control, pratyahara=withdrawal of senses, dharana=concentration, dhyana=meditation, samadhayah=contemplation, absorption or superconscious state, ashta=eight, angani=limbs or part

The eight limbs that constitute Raja Yoga are:

1. Yama (abstinence)
2. Niyama (observance)
3. asana (posture)
4. pranayama (breath control)
5. pratyahara (sense withdrawal)
6. dharana (concentration)
7. dhyana (meditation)
8. Samadhi (contemplation)

30. Ahimsa Satyasteya Brhamacaryaparighraha Yama

Ahimsa=non-violence, satya=truthfulness, asteya=non-stealing, brahmacharya continence, aparigraha=non-greed

The first limb of Ashtanga Yoga is called the Yamas. You need to remember that each of the eight limbs is equal to the others and necessary on your path. The first of the Yamas, or observances, is Ahimsa.

Ahimsa means "not causing pain". Some authors translate it as "non-killing" but it is more than just that. Himsa means "to cause pain", and ahimsa, is the opposite. To cause someone pain through words could be just as harmful as killing them; such as slander or libel. Even cruel words and thoughts can cause someone pain.

Satyam means "truthfulness"; not lying. Steyam means "not-stealing". Dr. Rao commented that these things seem so elementary but are, at the same time "elephantary." They are important and difficult to perfect. Brahmacharya is the practice of celibacy by those who are not married. The last limb or yama is aparigraha, which has been defined in two ways. One is "non-hoarding"—, not being greedy, not accumulating beyond our capacity to use things in a proper way. The other is not accepting gifts because they could just be a present for a future obligation.

The five principles are discussed further in Sutras 35–39.

31. Jati Desa Kala Samyanavacchinnah Sarvabhabhauma Mahavratam

Jati=class, desa=place, kala=time samaya=circumstance, anavachchinnah=not limited by, sarvahbhaumah=universal. mahavratam=great vows

These Great Vows are universal, not limited by class, place, time or circumstance.

Patanjali calls these the "mahavratam", or "great vows", because they can never be broken by any excuse: not by place, purpose, or social caste, not by winter, summer, morning, or evening or by this country or nationality. They are not commandments. These vows are for full-time dedicated Yogis. For people beginning Yoga, these vows can be modified according to their position in life—just like not all Roman Catholics are celibate only the Priests and Nuns.

32. Sauca Samtosa Tapah Svadhhya Yesvarapranidhanani Niyamah

Saucha=purity, samtosha=contentment, tapah=accepting pain and not causing pain, svadyaya=study of spiritual books, Isvarapranidhannani=worship of God or self-surrender, niyamah=observances

Niyama consists of purity, contentment, accepting but not causing pain, pain, study of spiritual books and worship of God (self-surrender).

The next limb, niyama, concerns observances. The five points in the yamas, together with the five points of the niyamas, are similar to the Ten Commandments of the Christian and Jewish faiths, as well as the Ten virtues of Buddhism. In fact, there is no religion without these moral or ethical codes. They are the foundation stones without which we can never build anything lasting-such as spiritual life.

33. Vitarka Badhane Pratipaksa Bhavanam

Vitarka=negative thoughts, badhane=when disturbed by, prattipaksha opposite thoughts, bhavanam=should be thought of

When disturbed by negative thoughts, opposite (positive) ones should be thought of. This is "pratipaksha bhavana".

In this Sutra, Patanjali teaches us how to control anger by taking our minds off what is disturbing us and redirecting it to another thought. This can be achieved in a number of ways. The most successful way is to go to people we love, then the thoughts of anger or hatred of a person who has caused a disturbance to our mind-lake will subside. The reason being is that you can not love and hate at the same time. The love produced by being with others will eventually overcome the hatred for anger of someone who has crossed you, got in your way or attempted to harm you.

34. Vitarka Himsadayah Krta Karitanumodita Lobha Krodha Moha Purvaka Mrdu Madhyadhimatra Duhkha Jnanananta Phala Iti Pratipaksa Bhavanam

Vitarka=negative thoughts, himsadayah=violence, etc., krita=done, karita, caused to be done, anumoditah=approved, lobha=greed, krodah=anger, moha infatuation, purvakah=preceded by, mridu=mild, madhya=medium,adhimarah, intense, duhkha=pain, ajana=ignorance, ananta=infinite, phalah=fruit, iti=thus, pratipaksa=opposite thoughts,bhavanam=should be thought of

When negative thoughts or acts such as violence, etc., are (committed) or even approved of, whether incited by greed, anger or infatuation, whether indulged in with mild, medium or extreme intensity, they are based on ignorance and can bring certain pain. Reflecting on a positive thought is also "pratinakasha bhavanam". To be able to redirect your thoughts from negative thoughts to positive thoughts.

Starting with Sutra 2.35, Patanjali covers the ten virtues one by one.

35. Ahimsa Pratishtayam Tat Smnidhau Vaira Tyagah

Ahimsa=non-violence, pratishthayam=having established, tat=in his, samnidhau=presence, vaira=hostility, tyagah=given up.

In the presence of one firmly established in non-violence, all hostilities cease.

When the vow of ahimsa is established in someone, all hatred of enemies ceases in his or her presence, because that person emits harmonious vibrations. If two people who have hatred or even ill feelings between them come to such a person, they will temporarily forget it. That is the benefit of ahimsa. When it is practiced, through thought, word and deed for a sustained period of time, the practitioner's entire personality brings out those vibrations.

36. Satya Pratisthayam Kriya Phalasr Yatvam

Satya=truthfulness, Pratishthayam=having established, Kriya=actions, Phala=fruits or results, asrayatvam=become subservient

To one established in truthfulness, actions and their results become subservient.

By establishing truthfulness, Yogis get the power to attain for themselves and others the fruits of work without doing the work. In other words, things come to them automatically. All nature loves an honest person. You will find that you need not run after things, for they will run after you. And if you are always truthful, if no lie comes from your mouth, a time will come when all you say will come true. Even if you say something by mistake, it will happen, because by practice of satayam the words become so powerful and clean that honesty becomes you. It wants to be with you always. If a curse is spoken, it will happen. If a blessing is said, it will happen. The more we lead a life of honesty, the more we will see the results, and that will in turn encourage us to be more honest.

37. Asteya Pratisthayam Sarva Ratno Upathanam

Asteya=non-stealing, pratishthayam=having established, sarva=all the, ratna=gems or wealth, upathanam=approaches, comes

To one established in non-stealing, all wealth comes.

38. Brhamacharya=continence, pratishtayam=having established, virya=vigor, labhah=gained

You can gain vigor and vitality by sexual continence.

39. Aparigraha Sthairye Jammakathamta Sambodhah

Aparigraha=non-greed, sthairye=confirmed, jammakatha=how and why of birth, sambodhah=thorough illumination

When non-greed is confirmed, a thorough illumination of the how and why of one's birth comes.

Aparigraha is abstention from greed or hoarding, which is a form of stealing or not receiving gifts. Many times we get gifts that are merely an advance for a future obligation. Someone will give us something expecting something in return. A donation is something given just for the sake of giving, not for name, money or publicity.

Dr. Rao says that accepting gifts binds us and makes us lose our neutrality. The mind will say, "You received a gift from him. How can you say something against him?" On the other hand, if we are strong enough to remain free of obligation, we can accept gifts. If you can feel, "I am giving her an opportunity to use her money in the right way, but I am not obligated by this gift. She should not come to me tomorrow out of obligation." Then we are not bound.

40. Sauchat Svanga Jugupsa Parair Amsargah.

Sauchat=by purification, svanga=for one's own body, jugupsa=disgust, parair=with others, asamsargah=cessation of contact.

By purification arises disgust for one's own body and for contact with other bodies.

When saucha, or purity, is observed, it makes you feel that even your own body is impure. We should not neglect our bodies by not combing our hair and not brushing our teeth, for instance, but we do not have to spend hours a day adoring it. You can relate this Sutra also to the practicing physical postures only to look attractive to others.

41. Sattvasuddhi Saumanasyaikagryenriya jayatmadarsana Yoghatvani Ca

Sattvasuddhi=purity of sattva, saumanazya=cheerfulness of mind, ekagrya=one-pointedness, indriyajaya=mastery of senses, Atmadarasana=realization of the Self, yoghatvani=fitness, cha=and

Moreover, one gains purity of sattva (tranquility), cheerfulness of mind, one-pointedness, mastery over the senses, and fitness for Self-realization.

Purification of the heart follows an understanding of the body. When the heart is pure, you are always happy. Concentration of the mind comes automatically, without you even trying. Only an impure mind runs to here and fro, forcing us to repeatedly to bring it back. All the senses are controlled too, and then comes *Atma darsana yogyatvani*—fitness for Self-Realization, or the vision of the Atma. These are all benefits of following Niyama's first observance—purity. Be pure in thought word and deed.

42. Samtosad Anuttamah Sukha Labhah

Samtosthat=by contentment, anuttamah=supreme, sukha=joy, lobhah=gained.

By contentment, supreme joy is gained.

As a result of contentment, one gains supreme joy. However it should be noted that, there is a difference between contentment and satisfaction. Contentment involves being as we are, and not looking to external things for our happiness. If something comes, we let it come. If it does not come so be it. Contentment means neither to like nor to dislike.

43. Kayedriya Siddhir Assuddhi Ksayat Tapash Savadhyad Istadevata Samprayog

Kaya=body, indriya=senses, siddhi=occult powers, asuddhi=impurities, kshayat=due to destruction, tapash=austerities

By austerity, impurities of body and senses are destroyed and occult powers gained.

The word "occult" can mean "mysterious" in this context. Even the practitioner may not be able to understand the powers or how they received them.

44. Savkhyayad=by study of spiritual books, Ishatadevata=chosen deity, samprayoga=communion

By study of spiritual books comes communion with one's chosen deity.

Once again; Patanjali explains that we should study the scriptures of the personal spiritual path into which we have been initiated. Svadhaya, or spiritual study, means study of scriptures, and also of any practice that is our own personal sadhana into which we have been initiated. Regular practice becomes study. Through that study, we receive Ishtadevata saprayogh—the vision, or darsan (instrument of seeing), of the Lord. Through constant effort, we get a vision of our chosen deity. In other words, each name has a form. If we stick to a certain word, eventually the form will appear automatically. It may come as a human form (e.g. an angel), a light or a sound.

### 45. Samadhi Siddhir Isvarapranidhanat

Samadhi=contemplation, siddir=attainment, Isvarapradidhant=by total surrender to God

By total surrender to God, samadhi is attained.

Isvara pranidhanam is a life of dedication, of offering everything to the Lord or to Humanity. What is humanity but a creation of the Infinite Supreme Being? For thousands of years, the Hebrews offered sheaths of wheat, grapes, or wine made from the grapes on an altar, as a sign of gratitude for successful crops. It was because of this familiar tradition that Christ used bread and wine at the Last Supper to connect His body and blood to his disciples. Where is God? Is He, She or It just sitting around somewhere waiting for us to give Him, Her, or It something directly? Giving to humanity is giving to God.

### 46. Sthira Sukham Asanam

Sthira=steady, sukham=comfortable, asanam=posture

Sana is a steady, comfortable posture

Asana has been defined as a posture that brings comfort and steadiness. Any pose that brings this comfort and steadiness is an asana. If you can achieve one pose, that is enough. It may sound easy, but achieving steadiness and comfort in even one pose is extremely difficult. It is very hard to sit in any particular position for any length of time without discomfort. Unless the body is free from all toxins and tensions, a comfortable pose is not easily obtained. When you are stressed, you will suffer stiffness and tensions. Only if we are supple will we not break.

### 47. Prayatna Saithilyananta Samapattibyam

Prayatna=natural tendency for restlessness, saithilya=by lessening, ananta=SamapatiBhyam=meditaing on

By lessening the natural tendency for restlessness and by meditating on the infinite; a posture is mastered. Because the pleasure we derive from, of our senses, we want to taste many things. Many of these things contain toxins, and they should be consumed in moderation. You can achieve steadiness by meditating on the infinite, or on the words of your Saints and Sages.

48. Tato Dvanvanabhighatah

Tato=thereafter, dvanva=by the dualities, anabhighatah=undisturbed

Thereafter, one is undisturbed by the dualities.

If you make the posture firm and comfortable, you will not be affected by anything—not blessings or curses, heat or cold, profit or loss. You will be in a state of neutrality. Shedding tears and feeling anger are acceptable, as long as it controlled by you and not by outside forces.

49. Tasmin Sati Svasa Prasasayor Gati Vicchedah Pranayamah

Tasmin=that, sati=being acquired, svasa=inhalation, prasvasayor=and exhalation, gati=movements, vicchedah=control,=pranayama

After mastering the posture, you must practice control of prana (vital breath) by controlling the motions of inhalation and exhalation. The Mayo Sports Clinic has shown that by the time you are 80 years old you will lose 40 percent of your lung capacity. This is from disuse of the muscles around your lungs. The more shallow you breath, the shallower of a breather you become. The oxygen needed for cells to be replenished will be lacking, a state which only accelerates the aging process. Doctors have shown that, while under narcotics, your body becomes more flexible. With proper breath control, you calm your mind and cause your body to become more flexible. Then, you can surrender into your postures rather than forcing yourself into them, thereby reducing the need for outside stimuli.

Pranayama does not involve holding your breath until your nerves are strained. It is gentle, slow, fully controlled breathing, without agitation and retention of breath. First start without retaining your breath at the end of inhale and also at the other end of the cycle of expelling the breath. The purpose is manifold. Concentrating on your breath, removes distractions, calms your mind, makes you flexible and prepares you ready for concentration, meditation and contemplation. While all eight parts of Raja Yoga are equal to one another. Some Yoga Practitioners, including myself, believe that Pranayama is the most important. Without Pranayama it is difficult to achieve Dharana, Dhyana, Samadhi or concentration, meditation, and contemplation.

50. Bahyabhyantara Stambha Vrittir Desakala Samkhyabhih Paridrsto Dighassuksmah

Bahya=external, abhyantara=internal, stambha=stationary, vrittir, modification, desa=space, kala=time, samkhayabhih=and number, paridristo=regulated, dirgha=long, sukshmah=short

The modifications of the life-breath are external, internal or stationary. They are to be regulated by space, time and number, and are either long or short.

In this Sutra, Patanjali talks about retention of breath either on the exhalation or inhalation. One should be very careful about retention, however. It should be practiced properly under personal supervision; you should never go beyond what a teacher tells us. The prana is very powerful energy.

Yoga Science identifies three basic types of pranayamas: bahya reite, abhyantara vritti and stambha vrite. Normally, in pranayama we teach only inward retention of the breath; this is easy and safe. After we have experienced the benefit of that sort of retention, we can practice outward retention.

51. Bahyabhyantara Visayaksepi Caturthath

Bahya external, abhyantara=internal, Visaya=object, akshepi=a form of concentration, Caturthath=the fourth

There is a fourth kind of pranayama that occurs while concentrating on an internal or external object.

52. Tatah Ksiyate Prakasavaranam

Tatah=as a result, kshiyate=destroyed, prakasa=light, avaranam=veil

In this section Patanjali discusses the benefit of pranayama. Prakasa, the light within us all, is covered by mental darkness. We use Pranyama to destroy the veil that covers the light. It cannot be removed by a magic wand. It must be removed one thread at a time until it no longer exists.

Patanjali states that the mind can be thought of as a veil woven of thoughts. It has no substance by itself. If we pull our thoughts out one after the other, there will be no mind left. One can make the analogy; it is like a heap of sugar. If we remove each grain of sugar one grain at a time, one after the other, the heap no longer exists once all the grains are gone.

As long as we continue to identify ourselves with the body we are mortal and not immortal. Pranayama helps us to understand the Oneness, the never changing one, because it removes the veil. It is not an easy practice but its rewards are enticing. Very few people come to meditation class, but thousands come for asanas and pranayama.

> 53. Dharanasu=for concentration, cha=yogyata=becomes first, manasah=mind
>
> If the prakasa avarana is removed, although the mind is not completely annihilated, its density is reduced and it becomes more capable of practicing dharana.
>
> 54. Sva Visayasamprayoge Citta-svarupanukara Ivendriyam Pratyaharah
>
> Sva=their own, vishaya=objects, asamprayoga=withdrawal, chitta-svarpupa=nature of the mind-composite, anukara=imitate, iva=as it were, indriyanam=senses, pratyaharah=abstraction
>
> When the senses withdraw themselves from the objects and imitate, as it were, the nature of the mind-composite, this is pratyahara.

However beneficial, practicing pranayama will not perfect the mind. There will always be distractions to the mind-composite that try to pull the mind to and fro, distractions that come from sensory perceptions. Seeing a nice car or a great-looking outfit will lead the mind to distraction.

No amount of pranayama, or controlled breathing, will stop those types of thoughts. You may stand in front of some desirable material thing practicing controlled breathing all day long; in the end it is your mind that has to put on the brakes.

Pratayhara is another way of controlling the mind and gaining mastery over your sense organs. You might be able to stand on your head for 20 minutes. You can practice your asanas for years and still be unable to control your senses. Even after years of practice you can still slip.

The Bhagavad-Gita says, "Yoga is not for the person who eats a lot or for one who starves. Yoga is not for the person who sleeps too much or for one who is always keeping vigil." We should not practice extremes, we should have reasonable limitations.

55. Tatah=thence, parama vasyata=supreme mastery, indreyanam=senses

Then follows supreme mastery over the senses.

By the proper practice of pratyahara, your senses come fully under your control. The senses become an obedient vehicle, taking you wherever you want. You become a complete master over them.

# INTRODUCTION TO CHAPTER THREE: VIBHUTI PADA—ON ATTAINMENT

Chapter Three deals with psychological analysis and supernatural powers. Some may question the validity of these powers, yet most people have read the minds of someone they have known for an extended period of time—a long time friend, a spouse, and a child. However, the ability to read a mind may not be reliable in every circumstance. The criteria projected to the receiver may not be accurate, and the purity of the receiving mind, may make the action less than pure, so it would be impossible to read someone's mind consistently. Instead of actually reading someone's mind, the receiver would be acting on instinct, which is the result of a pattern of "Samskaras" (memories) and past experiences created by that person and observed by the receiver. Every mother for example, has read the mind of her child. The motive for reading the child's mind was not selfish. There are countless accounts of a mother experiencing the feeling that a loved one is in danger, feeling pain or even envisioning death from a great distance. This Chapter also explains how this power is obtained.

What is so controversial about the second section of the third chapter is that Patanjali is only explains how a number of these attainments are achieved. He never actually tells the reader to go out and use them. He explains to you how powerful the mind can become through the regular practice of Yoga, but says these powers should only be used to assess your progress toward Super-Conscious Bliss.

This entire chapter is adopted from the Yoga adept Sri Sankara. Unfortunately, Sri Sankara did not give the word-to-word translation of Sanskrit to English that appears in the other three chapters. I want to mention this, since the format changes. The transliteration appears inside the commentary.

I have modified every paragraph, so I do not use quotation marks in this chapter. I received a grade of "A" from my examiner on my knowledge of the points in Sri Sankaras commentary and I do not believe that I changed the meaning he made in his original commentary. Sutras 3. 9–15 have left many people scratching their heads; however, after Sutras 1.2 and 1.3 these are the most important. They provide step by step instructions on how to achieve absolute oneness with the Infinite Universe, a oneness known as Super-Conscious Bliss.

I have removed some unnecessary words for you so the knowledge can flow to you unobstructed. I have also added some commentaries of my own from a Christian perspective. However I should add, I am in no way trying to convert anyone to Catholicism or to Christianity. I am only trying to do my duty and to propagate Yoga Science to Westerners who come from predominantly Judeo-Christian backgrounds.

Om Shanti shanty

God, Peace, Peace

# Chapter 3

▼

# VIBHUTI PADA—ON ATTAINMENT

1. Desha—Badhaschittasya Dharana

Dharana is the act of holding or focusing attention within a limited area of concentration; usually a particular or general place.

Dharana, or concentration, is when the mind holds onto some object either in the body or outside the body, thereby keeping the mind in that state. When the mind focuses with eyes open on an external object it is called Trataka Dharana. The other type of Dharana is focusing one's attention within. Inside your body are innumerable areas of concentration. For convenience, Yoga has classified seven fundamental nerve plexuses, called Chakras: Muladhara Bhu, which includes the lowest part of the abdomen and the genital organs; Svadhistana Bhuvah, includes both legs and the lower abdomen. Mannipura Svah, includes all abdominal organs; Anahata Manah, which includes all anatomical organs of the chest; Visuddha Janah, which includes the neck, the gateway of life; Ajan Tapah, which comprises sensor and motor station of the central nervous system except the cerebral cortex, and Shasraram Satyam, includes cerebrum, cerebellum and cerebral cortex. When one of these Chakras is selected for concentration it is called particular Dharana fixation. All external concentrations with the eyes open are considered Trataka concentration.

2. Tatara Pratyaikatanata Dhyanam

"When there is an unbroken flow of knowledge towards the object, this is known as Dhyana." The undisturbed, continuous flow of this mental effort is meditation.

When the mind tries to think of only one object—by holding itself to one particular spot—and succeeds in receiving sensations only through that part of the body, this is known as Dharana. When the mind succeeds in keeping itself in that state for an extended period of time, it is called Dhyana.

   3. Tat-Eva-arthamatra Nirhasam Svarupa-Hunyam Iva Sadadhih

"When that giving up all forms reflects only the meaning, it is Samadhi."

Trance consciousness occurs when, through the same mental effort as Dharana and Dhyana, the object of meditation shines alone and reveals itself, which is the nature of self-cognition. This cognitive form of meditation occurs when the mind absorbs the nature of an object free from all distracting thoughts. When the true meaning of the suggested object shines forth, as it were, apart from its external form of the object, and the remaining part gives up its form through constant continuation of suggestion, leaving nothing but the meaning, this is Samadhi.

   4. Trayam Ekatra Samyamah

"When fixation, suggestion and cognitive trance operate simultaneously this is called Samyama."

When a student of Yoga can direct his/her mind to any particular object and keep it there for a long time, separating the object from the internal part, this is Samyama, the process of Dharana, Dhyana and Samadhi, following one another and making one. The form of the object vanishes leaving only its meaning. Many times a beginner can only meditate after a teacher makes a vocal suggestion. Vocal suggestion is fitting when the mind is not able to concentrate. Vocal suggestion is especially used to suggest things to others. Sometimes, the student may see no perceivable result of the suggestion. However, for those in an advanced state these three work together in a moment. In this state, one does not need to separate them and it is almost impossible to do anyway. For instance, when a student directs his mind to a particular object, keeps it there for a long time, and then feels its suggested result, this is not Samyama. Only when they work simultaneously, is it then called Samyama, which is the result of advanced meditation.

Catholics, not to mention Episcopalians and Lutherans, believe that simple bread and wine becomes Christ before communion. They do not believe that it becomes the actual physical being of the carpenter from Nazareth but rather His True Presence. How does this actually occur? Patanjali may, and I don't want to be excommunicated so I want to strongly emphasize the word **may**, have given the actual mechanics of how this occurs 200 years before Christ. Allow me to construct this analogy: the congregation focuses on the bread and wine thus illustrating a type of concentration, or Dharana. Through vocal suggestions of the presider (priest or pastor), there is continuous flow of knowledge into the objects, a flow quite similar to meditation or Dhyana. Then when nothing is left but the objects true meaning, there is Samadhi, or a Super-Conscious State of contemplation. When all three occur simultaneously, this is Samyama.

Likewise, in Yoga when the aforementioned three states,—concentration, meditation and supreme contemplation—are directed towards Purusha (in this context the Supreme Soul), also the highest Bliss is also obtained. In the case of the Christian congregations who all consider themselves sinners and weak, the ritual must be performed on a daily, weekly or monthly basis. So, too, the Yogi does not stay in the highest form of Bliss while living in this World. Buddha was said to return to his *Center* twice a day. No one reaches perfection while in a human form. The soul is in a constant state of purification.

5. Taj-Jayat Prajana-Lokah

By the conquest of that (Samyama) comes light of knowledge.

The achievement of Samyama produces clarity of cognition and consciousness. With mastering Samyama comes the light of intuitive knowledge, an achievement that brings direct perception of truth regarding the object. When the student has succeeded in achieving this Samyama, all powers come under his control. This is a great instrument of the Yogi. The objects of knowledge on which to perform Samyama are infinite and they are divided into gross, grosser and grossest by stages, and are finally brought to the more subtle things. As Samyama becomes deeper and deeper, so the trance of cognition Samadhi Prajna becomes more and more lucid.

6. Tasyu Bhumishu Viniyogah

Their application (of Samyama) is to discover the gradated planes (or stages) of consciousness.

In this Sutra Patanjali warns us not to attempt to go too fast. When Samyama conquers one plane of consciousness it is applied to the next immediately following plane. A student who has not even conquered the lower planes of consciousness certainly cannot yet conquer the higher planes. When you concentrate on Purusha (the Supreme Soul or God), you need not worry about planes. It in itself is the highest state, and it includes all beauty, all love, all existence, all knowledge—and the universe itself. Experience of the higher state of Samadhi cannot be put into words and pictures; it can only be experienced by the Chitta (mind-composite) alone. Through the practice of Yoga, the experience of Yoga must be gained. Experience is the teacher of higher experience in Yoga. He who knows this secret remains in the State of Cosmic Consciousness forever.

### 7. Trayam Antarangam Purvebhyah

"These three are more internal than those that precede."

These three—Daharana, Dhyana and Samadhi—constitute the internal accessories, intrinsic Yoga, in comparison with the previous five—which are—Pratyahara, Pranayama, Asana, Yama and Niyama (which were explained in detail in Sutras 2.35–2.53)

First, one has to discover Pratyahara, Pranayama, Asana, Yama and Niyama the external parts of the three; Dharana, Dhyana and Samadhi. When a person has attained them, he may then attain to omniscience (being all present) and omnipotence (being all-powerful). However gaining omniscience and omnipotence is not salvation. These three would not make the mind Nirvikalpa, changeless, but would leave the seeds for getting bodies again. Only when the seeds are "fried" do they lose the possibility of producing further plants. These powers cannot fry the seeds, cannot destroy them completely.

### 8. Tad-Api Bahirangan Nirbejasya

"But even they are external to the seedless samadhi."

Even this internal triad of means become external to the seedless Samadhi.

Until we reach the highest form of Samadhi, we exist in a lower stage, in which the Universe still exists as we see it. The intimate trio of meditation becomes a means in the state of Asamprajnata Samadhi, because its aim is accomplished before seedless Samadhi. On the other hand Neerbeja Samadhi, concentration, meditation and cognition control the meditators individuality. Although they are indirectly helpful (the intimate trio), they are still only external and an indirect means to the ultimate goal. No further suggestion is needed when Purusha (the Supreme Soul) is realized directly. A vehicle is unnecessary for one who "enters the house". The purpose is to bring one to the entrance of one's destination. To realize the True self, which is God (Purusha), the minds-composite with its senses turns into the Cosmic Ultimate Reality or One without second. Having reached a higher state, a Yoga student begins to receive cosmic suggestions, and his individual suggestions gradually cease.

9. Vyuthana-Nirodha-samskarayorabhibhava-Pradurbhavaunirodha-Kshana Chittanvayo Nirodha-Parinamah

By suppressing the disturbed impressions of the mind, and by the rise of impressions of control, the mind will persist in that moment of control and will attain a controlling modification.

This creates a conjunction of mind-composite (Chitta) to a moment of restraint (nirodha). A concentrated mind becomes identical with Cosmic Chittam, which is manifested at the moment of complete concentration.

Consequently, the destructive instinctual driving psychic forces will disappear, and constructive driving forces will be manifested. In short, in the first state of Samadhi, the modifications of the mind have been controlled. However if they are controlled perfectly there is no need for a modification. Hence, another checks one wave. Until there are no waves, you have not reached Perfect Samadhi—although the lower Samadhis will get you to the doorway.

10. Tasya Prashanta-Vahita Samskarat

"Its flow becomes steady by habit."

The undisturbed flow of disappearing and appearing is a process dependent upon the root potentials of both. Due to its inherent purity, the stream of Cosmic Consciousness flows peacefully, calmly and blissfully.

The flow of this continuous control of the mind becomes steady with daily practice and the mind obtains the faculty of constant concentration.

11. Sarvarthatikagratayoh Kshayodayau Chittasya Samadhi-Prarinamah

"Taking in all sorts of objects and concentrating upon one object, these two powers will be destroyed."

Manifested respectively, the chitta is the destruction of these powers, the common all-pointedness (scattering mind) and the Yogic one-pointedness (concentrated mind) respectively. When the mind-composite reaches the state of Samadhi, the multiplicity of the universe is destroyed, and its unity emerges.

Multiplicity creates all-pointedness, which allows the mind to wander dualistically towards objects or subjects randomly without direction. Dissatisfaction, disappointment, frustration and anxiety arise if those various satisfactions are not gained by the mind-composite. Unity creates one-pointedness, (Ekagrata), in the mind, and when the duality disappears, the result is satisfaction, peace, happiness and serenity.

The inherent cause of Sarvarthata (Sarva, all+Arthata, pointed) is the multiplicity of the objective universe. The cause of Ekagrata (Eka, one+Agarta, pointedness) is when one obtains the knowledge that the one principle which pervades the universe is that the Supreme Consciousness manifests itself in various forms and names. If one believes that Samadhi is Cosmic Consciousness, then all-pointedness disappears in the absence of its cause, multiplicity, and is replaced by the unity of the manifested universe. When the mind-composite reaches the state of Samadhi, (Cosmic Consciousness), all-pointedness disappears in the absence of its cause, multiplicity, and is replaced by one-pointedness, which is the prevailing characteristic of the Cosmic Mind. The destruction of all-pointedness results from the absence of its cause, materiality. The rise of one-pointedness is marked by its appearance in the presence of its causes, unity and spirituality. When the mind recognizes that it is approaching the spiritual, and eventually finds that spirit, it becomes transcendent and imminent. The mind will then leans towards Samadhi, Cosmic Consciousness. (As this becomes closer to reality the students of Yoga need not worry). Experiencing Samadhi destroys multiplicity and all-pointedness, and that destruction will bring out unity and one-pointedness in the mind. Constant, continuous concentration brings about the state, of supreme concentration (Nirodha), in which the total mind is restrained. This Nirodha (restraint) transforms the mind into a perfect Samadhi. In short, the mind usually takes in various objects constantly without the ability to shut them out. This is the lower state. Then there is the higher state of the mind, when the mind takes up one object and excludes all others, of which Samadhi is the result.

12. Tatah Punah Shantoditau Tulay-Pratyayau Chittasyatikagrata-Parinamah

One-pointedness of the mind occurs when past and present impressions that are similar. Moreover, when the subsiding and rising cognitive impulses are precisely similar, the mental modifications become one-pointed. When the mind-composite reaches the beginning of a one-pointed state, the past and present impressions becomes similar.

When do we know that the mind has become concentrated? When the idea of time has vanished. The more time passes unnoticed, the more concentrated we become. In everyday life when we are interested in a book or a piece of music, we do not notice our surroundings at all, and when we leave that activity we are often surprised to find out how much time has passed. Time has the tendency to stand in the one present. So the explanation that has been given when the past and present come and stand in one is that the mind is concentrated. Change is the universal law and has no exception. In the state of Samadhi and one-pointedness, these changes are similar, continuously closer to Self-Realization. Thus in Samadhis the idea of time and space disappear. The mind is naturally beyond time, space, cause, effect, and person. When it is concentrated, it goes not to its real nature, but beyond a casual state. The more time passes unnoticed, the more the mind is concentrated. This state is beyond time, due to the eternal presence of mind, and it is always in the present. Consciousness is always in the present, the past is the part of memory and future is the part of planning. When consciousness passes on, its previous experience is called ("Shanta", subsided or "past"), and future, Udita. How it arises in the present and future are indicative of relativity or dissimilarity. During Samadhi dissimilarity disappears; for this reason relativity, since it depends on the notion of dissimilarity, it also disappears.

Similarity means not absolute sameness, but sameness of nature, otherwise, higher and higher experiences would not be possible. All lights including sunlight are similar in the respect that they are luminous; however they are not similar in respect to heat and intensity. So too in Samadhi, when similar ideas arise, they do not mean repetition of the same ideas, but sameness in a meritorious way. They are constantly higher and higher and are beyond the confines of language. They can be experienced, but cannot be described in words. They can be taught and indicated only to those that have had similar experiences. These experiences will go higher and higher until Ultimate Reality, Purusha, is realized; then, one sees the multiplicity of the universe in the unity of God, and the unity of God in the multiplicity of the universe. Purusha is Pure Existence, Pure Consciousness and Pure Bliss. This is the ultimate aim of meditation. Nothing is beyond Purusha, and he who experiences it is called a liberated one.

13. Etena Butendriyeshu Dharma-Lakshana-Avastha-Parinama Vyakhyatah

"By this is explained the three-fold transformation of form, time and state in fine or gross matter and in the organs."

These are the changes in nature, the characteristic and physical condition with regard to the objective and instrumental phenomena. In explaining the changes in the Chittam, the changes in property, secondary characteristics and state regarding elements, body and senses are also explained.

The changes both in our consciousness and also in matter are innumerable; however, Patanjali places them into three categories: Dharma Parinama, Lakshana Parinama and Avasta Parinama. When a substance that is endowed with a property leaves its home property and embraces another property this is called Dharma Parinama. When clay leaves its property of lumpiness and assumes another form such as a jar, the change the clay has undergone is called Dharma Parinama.

When the same jar leaves its present form and is no longer visible in that present form because of time this is called Lakshana Parinama. A statue potentially exists in a piece of marble, just like the jar potentially exists in the clay. However it is only manifested after the superfluous parts of the base substance are removed. Both forms exist in the future before they become visible.

If the jar or statue erodes because of the passing of time, that change is Avasta Parinama. Every moment, the molecules that make up the statue or the jar are changing but you do not notice it at any one moment because of the subtlety of the change—because it happens very slowly. It does not exist even for one moment without a change taking place. Infancy, childhood, youth, maturity and old age of a human are another example of Avasta Parinama.

Although a lump of sugar placed in a glass of water changes its white and hard form, it can still be recognized through its sweet taste. The change of matter into solid, liquid and gas is another instance of physical change where only the form of the original substance is changed; this type of change is known as Dharma Parinama. Lakshana Parinama is a chemical change, in which the actual composition of the original substance is altered; for instance,where the original substance disappears and a new substance is formed, such as in appearance of ash from a burnt paper and the formation of animal tissues from vegetable substances. Avasta Parimanma is a change of state, such as change of ice into water and then into steam when exposed to heat.

The changes described by Patanjali's Sutras are examples of Dharma Parinama, in which the whole conscious state of the mind is altered, but because they are on the unconscious or subconscious level, these causes are latent. When your conscious and subconscious mind changes; your whole personality, which is the cause of past, present and future is altered, it is an example of Laskshana Parinama. Referring back to the Sutras 9, 11,and 12 when the mind-composite starts changing as result of Vrittis (modifications), it also changes its form. As a result, when consciousness passes through past, present and future moments, the change is a result of time. The causation of the impressions will vary in intensity within one particular period. Although you are in the present, your conscious state is changing.

The concentrations taught in the preceding Sutras are intended to give the student a voluntary control over the transformations of their mind-composite, which alone will enable them to create Samyama (simultaneous concentration, meditation and contemplation) referred to in the fourth Sutra of this chapter.

The distinction among the three kinds of concentrations mentioned in Sutras 9,11, and 12 is as follows: in the first, the disturbed impressions are merely held back, but they are not altogether obliterated by the impressions of control which just come in; in the second, the former impressions of control are completely suppressed by the later which stand in bold relief; while in the third, which is the highest, there is no question of suppressing, but only similar impressions succeeding each other in a stream. Thus when subjective self-consciousness changes from multiplicity to union with the Supreme, there is a similar change in sense, sensation and perception as well as in the elemental universe. The change from gross to finer happens as a consequence of Dharma Parinama. When subjective self-consciousness is submerged in Purusha (true self which is God), multiplicity of the senses and of the elemental universe become submerged in the subject, Purusha, as a consequence of change because of time which is the characteristic of Lakshana Parinama. When the subjective and objective universe are transformed into Purusha, it progressively changes into nothing but a Pure Stream of Consciousness as a consequence of Avasta Parinama. This is similar to the transformation of ice to water to steam.

14. Shatdhavyapadesha-Dharmanupah Dharmi

That which is acted upon by transformation—either past, present or yet to be manifested—is the qualified. The object characterized conforms to the latent (past), the rising (present), and the unpredictable,(future characteristics). A substance, substratum (layer underneath) or Dharmi, is that which consists of a property in all its states, whether they are Shata, (disappeared), Unita, (manifested), or Avapadeshay, (unpredictable or yet to be manifested).

Shantas are those properties that have accomplished their respective functions and entered the past, (Atita). Unitas are those properties which have been fully manifested. Avyapadeshya are those properties which exist potentially and are waiting for manifestation. According to the philosophy of Sankhya-Yoga, there is no creation or destruction. There is only evolution and involution. All things are ultimately dissolved into Prakruti (nature), and all things are manifested again at the time of evolution.(At many funerals you may hear the phrase ashes to ashes dust to dust). Its force Shaktiis is called Dharma. Whatever is manifested is a physical form, a property whose force is still unknown. Existence of this force is inferred by the production of its specific result, the experience of touch and by the motion of objects in it. Of these characteristics, the present is in operation. The present character is different from those that are latent and those that are to be manifested, or those potentially exist also known as Avyapadeshya. Insofar as the common nature is not destroyed, every state includes the other state. The past contains the present and the future; in short, everything contains the essence of everything else.

However due to cause, effect, space and time, not every state is manifested at the same time. That which contains all things and all states, that which passes through a succession of the past, present and future, whether latent, manifested or unpredictable, that which is the substratum of both the generic form and the particular, and that which is present in all things but is different from the others is the substance Dharmin. Without something motionless, how could motion be detected? A Dharmi, (a subject or seer) must be free from perpetual modifications and movements of the physical manifold. A Dharmi must be a simple unitary and unchangeable substance. Nothing, whatever it is, can manifest itself in any other thing unless it existed there potentially in its cause. All this manifestation takes place in relation to the form; however, it is nothing but a new arrangement of the original three cosmic forces. The Gunas (qualities or characteristics) can never exist without forces and properties. Properties and qualities which have manifested themselves and have since passed into the subconscious level become latent deposits. They remain tranquil because they have played their part but they are still there to form personality and to become actively manifested at another time. The properties that are being manifested are active, while others not yet manifested are in the realm of possibility, as the indefinable and unpredictable. Thus the Dharmi (substrata) become correlated to the properties of past, present and future. A substance cannot be recognized without its properties. That is to say, the qualified is the substance which is being acted upon by time, however the Samskaras (memories) are constantly changing and being manifested every moment.

15. Kramanyatvam Parinamanyatve Hetuh

The succession of changes is the cause of manifold (multiplying) evolution. The distinctiveness of sequence is the reason for the distinctive sequence of manifestations. The entire material universe is made up of three particles of nature: electrons, protons and neutrons. Different orders and arrangements of these particles make a definite change in atoms, and the different orders in the arrangement of atoms make a definite change in molecules and compounds.

The fundamental particles of matter, such as electrons are limited in number, but out of these fundamental elements the innumerable objects of the universe are created. In whatsoever that anything may manifest itself, whenever there is a change in effect, it is due to the change of the order and arrangement of the cause. It may be a physical change (Dharma Parinama), or a chemical change (Lakshana Parinama), or merely a change of state Avasta Parinama. Whatever change occurs, the total energy of the universe remains the same. There is neither the creation nor destruction of matter. There is only the changing of energy and matter from one form to another. The universe is in a state of incessant change, which is the Ultimate Reality, Siva is the ultimate force. Prakruti, Shakti or Dharma are the only substances that are unchanged.

From the following Sutra to the end of the third chapter, the application of Samyama and its consequences, extrasensory perception, and supernatural powers are described. Until you are able to concentrate, meditate and contemplate simultaneously (Samyama) these will be difficult to achieve.

A friend of mine asked me, "Can you walk on water"? I told her, "I wouldn't tell you if I did; however, the apostle Peter walked on water, so I should have the ability to do it." The following Sutras explain the mechanics of how to achieve that supernatural power and others like it. You can download from the Internet instructions on how to make a nuclear weapon. It does not mean, however, you have the tools or resources to manufacture one, or a dark enough mind (kshipta) to detonate it. If you use these powers, do so at your own risk, and by all means, do not harm anyone.

### 16. Parinama-Traya-Samyamad Atita-Anagat-Jman

"By performing Samyama on the three sorts of changes comes the knowledge of past and future."

The present is already known because the meditator is working with his present consciousness. Their effects infer the causes and the effect can be inferred from their causes. Through the present, which is the cause of their future effect, one can know the future accurately.

If a person is suffering, they must have accumulated the causes of their misery. If a person is preoccupied with evil doings, they will positively suffer in the future. In short, if you rob convenience stores for a living, you must know your future is going to be unpleasant.

Likewise, if a person is happy and prosperous, they must have accumulated the cause of their prosperity and happiness. If a person engages in good and meritorious activities, he will have a prosperous and happy life. If a person is not getting expected results in their life, he should examine his subconscious mind to understand his past and to build his future according to their expectations.

A change in the cause will produce a definite change in the effect, as stated in Sutra 3.15. If a person is spiritually, mentally and physically happy and prosperous, he should understand his good past actions (Karmas) and he should increase his good actions (Karmas), for more happiness and prosperity in the future, by using Samyama on Dharma Parinama (physical change), Lakshana Parinama (character change) and Avasta Parinama (change of state). In the subjective and the objective worlds one discovers continuity. Consequently, past, present and future become known. For this reason one should analyze carefully the instinctual driving forces of the mind-composite, dream life, dreamless life and the meditative state. When the mind has attained a state of oneness—when it identifies itself with the internal impression of the object, leaving the external impression of the object behind through long practice, it is retained by the mind and the mind can get into that state of oneness, identifying itself with the internal impression of the object, leaving the external through long practice—this is Samyama. If a person in that state wants to know the past and future, he must practice a Samyama on the changes in the Samskaras (past impressions). Some are working at present, some have been worked out and some are waiting to work. So, by performing a Samyama on these, he knows the past and future.

17. Sabda-Artha-Pratyayanam-It aretara-Adhyasat-Samkaras-Pravi-Ghagat Samyamatsarva-Bhuta-Ruta-Jnam

By practicing Samyama on word, meaning and knowledge, which are intermingled, the knowledge of all animal sounds can be attained.

The word, the meaning and the impulse, appear as one, because each coincides with the other; by performing Samyama on their distinctiveness comes the knowledge of the sound of all living beings.

To understand the previous two Sutras, we have to understand certain fundamental principles that attempt to put into order and explain a body of hypotheses concerning human mental functioning and development—mind-consciousness, ego-consciousness and super consciousness can operate on the following planes: Conscious level, the dream and waking states; Unconsciousness or sub-conscious level; Super-consciousness level; or Samadhi. Mind or psychological consciousness is not the whole of the mind-composite, but only a partial manifestation of latent and sub-conscious impressions, desires and instincts. However, this psychological consciousness is not accidental or random. It is a systematic manifestation of the sub-conscious mind both qualitatively and quantitatively.

The two fundamental principles in use of Samyama are; (1) Psychic determination or causality, (2) Existence and significance of mental processes. The first principle means that in the mind, as in the physical nature around us, nothing happens by chance. Every mental event is determined by events which preceded it, although some may seem to be unrelated to what came before them. Discontinuity does not exist in mental life. Understanding the application of this principle is essential for proper orientation in the use of Samyama to know past, present and future. If we observe carefully and apply the principle correctly, we will never dismiss any mental phenomenon as meaningless and accidental. So-called illusions, delusions and even hallucinations are guiding lights to the unconscious or sub-conscious mind. We should carefully examine waking, dreaming, dreamless sleep and the meditative state. For every mental event, we should reflect on its cause. The cause lies in the sub-conscious mind, since that is where the phenomenon comes from. Whether we can discover it or not, the answer is there. A common psychological experience of every day life is to forget something or to make a mistake in one's work. A layman calls such an incident an accident or something "that just happened". But a thorough investigation of such phenomena will reveal a corresponding mental cause. So they are not merely accidents. Dream and dreamless sleep also have corresponding mental causes. Each dream, each imagination and each day's dreamless sleep are consequences of other mental events. What goes on in one's mind is unconscious, unknown to oneself; this is what accounts for the apparent discontinuity in one's mental life. Usually when a thought, a feeling, an image, an idea, an accidental forgetting, a mistake, a dream, or a pathological symptom seems to be unrelated to what went before it in the mind, it is because its casual connection is with some unconscious mental process rather than with a conscious one. If subconscious causes can be discovered, all apparent discontinuations disappear and the causal chain and sequence becomes clear.

It is extremely difficult to discover unconscious and subconscious mental processes. However you can, by performing Samyama, cognize them directly. The conscious state is determined by the subconscious state of your mind-composite, Chittam. By going into a deeper state of Samadhi, one directly cognizes the manifestation of Mudras and Yoga-Nidras; which are a manifestation of what has been called Kundalini, or "coiled power within". These Mudras and Yogandiras are a manifestation of a higher level of existence of the mind-composite. Gradually, from the storehouse of the subconscious mind, all feelings, ideas and wishes will come to the level of the conscious mind. One has to filter these feelings by supra-electronic forces, called Tanmatras and Gunas. When feelings resulting from past impressions are completely fried, the tranquil quality, which is Self-existent, Self-luminous and beyond relativity, is manifested. Due to the manifestation of this tranquil quality, of the mind-composite, a student of Yoga knows the past, present and future directly. Innumerable previous incarnations of past lives are hidden in the subconscious. Mental life is not discontinuous. Birth and death are not a beginning and end of mental life; they are however the beginning and end of one's biological life according to Yogic Science.

Without checking the past lives that make up the subconscious mind the present life cannot be improved and a better future life cannot be built. Thus a student of Yoga standing in the present should learn from the past, build a glorious present and plan a majestic future. When the student purifies his subconscious state of Chittam by using Samyama on Dharmi Parinama (physical change), Lakashana Parinama (character change), and Avasta Parinama, (change of state), on the subjective and the objective worlds, he discovers continuity. Consequently past, present and future become known. For this reason one should analyze carefully the instinctual driving forces of the psychic apparatus: Chittam, dream life, dreamless sleep, waking life the and meditative state.

In Sutra 17, the word represents the external cause, and the meaning represents the internal vibration that travels to the brain through the channels of senses, called Indriyas, which convey the external impression to the mind. Knowledge represents the reaction of the mind, from which comes perception. These three, when confused, make our sense-objects. Suppose we hear a word; there is first the external vibration, next the internal sensation. Ordinarily, these three are inseparable, but through the practice of Yoga we can separate them. When a person has attained this level and they practice Samyama on any sound, they can understand the meaning that sound was intended to express, regardless of whether it was made by a human or an animal.

You can tell when a female dog does not want you, even her master, near her newborn pup by her low growl. It is a warning; more than an aggressive growl, of a dog that doesn't want you on its master's property. You know when you are being lambasted by someone in a foreign language even if you do not really understand the exact words being uttered. Normally, sounds, sense and idea are all so intimately fused they are inseparable and are only presented to express knowledge that exists internally. We use words to convey our ideas and knowledge to others to whom we have no other method of expressing ourselves. Internal forces, which are revealed in the form of knowledge by means of word, meaning, idea, indication and various other symbols are called Sphota. By performing Samyama separately on word, meaning and idea, we gain the ability to comprehend all sounds knowledge of all sounds uttered by any living being in nature. It is a phenomenon of psychic mechanism and that can only be understood if that psychic mechanism is familiar with its uses. That is the reason one cannot understand a language one has not studied. Word, meaning and idea run into one another on account of mutual correlation or coincidence. Take for instance the word, "bird", the object "bird" and the idea "bird. The word, the meaning and the idea are separate from one another, but due to conventional use, we find the distinction difficult to believe. If we listen to a foreign language, which we do not know, we hear a word, but we do not know the meaning or the idea behind it. Word is one thing, meaning is another and idea is another. By performing Samyama on each one separately, one can obtain knowledge of the sounds of all living beings. In a deeper state of Samadhi, one is in direct communications with Sphota, which is the source of all knowledge.

### 18. Samskaras-Sakshatkaranat-Purva-Jatijmanam

With perceiving the impressions, comes the knowledge of past life.

By bringing out the root of our existence from its sub-conscious level into direct consciousness, the knowledge of previous life-states arises. By performing Samyama on the drives, one brings them to the level of consciousness; as a result, one knows one's own and even another's previous births. Each experience that we have comes in the form of a wave in the Chitta, which subsides and becomes finer and finer but is never lost. It remains there in minuscule form, and if we can dredge up this wave again, it becomes memory. So, if the student of Yoga can perform Samyama on these past impressions in the mind, he will begin to remember all his past lives. The two principles, psychic determinism or causality and the existence and significance of mental processes, form the groundwork on which knowledge of the previous incarnations and the next incarnation rests. They are guides that direct and determine our approach in performing Samyama to know all previous and subsequent lives.

### 19. Pratyayasya-Para-Chitta-Jmaanam

By performing Samyama on the signs in another's body, knowledge of his mind comes.

By observing carefully another person's impulses, the knowledge of their mind comes. That principle by which objects are known is called Prataya. By performing Samyama on the process of the psychic mechanism, *modus operandi* of mind-composite, there arises knowledge about another's mind.

Each person has particular mannerisms, which differentiate him from others. When the student of Yoga performs Samyama on these signs he knows the nature of the mind of that person. According to Samkhya Yoga, mind-composite, ego, and super-consciousness are eternal, and death and birth are the sunset and sunrise of the mind-composite. If one can know the laws of the mind and its nature, which are beyond time and space, one will know another's mind in the same way that one knows one's own mind. A perfect student of Yoga can read anyone's mind without difficulty. As I pointed out in the introduction to this chapter, the reading of the subject's mind is a case of direct perception as opposed to inductive and deductive inference, which may be true or false, depending on the methods adopted in examination.

VIBHUTI PADA—ON ATTAINMENT 79

20. Na Cha Tat Salambanam Tasya-Avishayi-Bhutatvat

Using Yoga, one can read another's mind not its contents; this not, after all, the object of this Samyama.

Using this intuitive knowledge of Samyama, it does not make it support the contents of the another persons mind because the aim and principle of this Samyama is to read the mind not identify with the contents of the other persons mind.

A student would not know the contents of the mind by performing this Samyama on the body. That would require a twofold Samyama, first on the signs in the body and then on the mind itself. The student would then know everything that is in that mind. The student of Yoga knows the minds of others without identifying with them, therefore he is unaffected by the suffering of the minds he reads.

Without identifying with the contents, the student can know the truth about another's life, even parts with which the that person is unfamiliar. It is identification with the body and the senses that causes persons to suffer. But Samyama is the identification with Purusha (supreme soul) only and not with the multiplicity of the Universe.

21. Kay-Rupa-Samyamat Tad-Grahya-Shakti-Stambhe-Chakshuh-Prakasha Asamprayoge Antar-dhanam

By performing Samyama on the form of the body, the perceptibility of the form being obstructed, and the power of manifestation in the eye being separated, the Yogi's body becomes invisible.

By performing Samyama on the physiological aspect of the body, the power of perceptibility—the light which carries it to the eye—is checked: then since there is no means of contact with the functional activity of the eye, the Yogi's body appears to vanish. By performing Samyama on the form and the color of the body, the perceptibility of the body can be checked and as a consequence of disjunction of the light from the body to the eyes of others, the power of disappearance will come.

By performing Samyama on the form and color of the body, the power of perceptibility of the form and color of the body is suspended. When light which is the medium of optical perception, does not reflect from a Yogi's body to the eyes of others, the Yogi will be out of contact with others and he is unseen due to his power of disappearance. A Yogi standing in the midst of people, may seem to disappear. No one sees him going and coming. The color and the form of the body are, as it were, separated. He does not really vanish but he cannot be seen by anyone. This can only be done when the Yogi has attained the power of concentration when the form and thing formed have been separated.

22. Etena Shabda-Dyantar-Dhanam Uktam

Using the same type of Samyama explained in the previous Sutra, disappearance or concealment of words being spoken and other such things, are explained.

By this (Samyama), one should understand the power of disappearance of attention from sound, touch, smell, taste, hearing etc.

It is the union of the body and the mind that brings material happiness or suffering, but neither alone can bring union. This union is achieved by means of sensory and motor organs. If the union of the mind (attention) is removed, there is no registration of that particular sensation of motion.

Once that union is achieved, pain and suffering will disappear. For instance, when a person has a constant ache or pain anywhere in his body, his aches and pains will disappear if he can remove his attention from that particular part of the body and from that sensation. Furthermore it is a common experience that the presence of beloved friends and relatives alleviates sufferings. Beginners cannot meditate in a noisy place, but if they practice Samyama on attention to all sounds, sound will be transformed into any general sensation. In the same way, any sensation of illness can be removed and transformed into any general sensation. Wonderful vision, smell, hearing, touch and taste can be created, and their bad forms can be destroyed by the practice of Samyama.

23. Sopa-Kraman Nirupa-Kramam Cha Karma Tat-Smayamad Apraranta
    Jmanam Aristebhyo Va

Karma is of two kinds, soon-to-fructified and late-to-be fructified. By performing Samyama on these, (certain signs called Aristas), portents or "omens" will occur and Yogis will know the exact time of separation from their bodies.

Karma, (action-complex) is either fast or slow in fruition, but by performing Samyama over these or the portents (omens), comes the knowledge of the proximity of death.

This is one of the more difficult Sutras to explain. Most people fear dying and the last supernatural power they would want to obtain is knowing exactly when that biological event occurs. (However, Christ was said to have known exactly when he was going to die and did not use any of his other powers to prevent that event from occurring).

By performing Samyama on Karmas which are either fast or slow in fruition, one obtains intuitive knowledge of death and extraordinary happenings. Karma that is the cause of life-state, lifetime and life experience, is of two kinds: Karma that is fast in fruition and Karma which is slow in fruition.

Life and death are two aspects for creative forces. Neither one of these aspects can stand without the other, so too is the process of life and death and vice-versa. The process of life and death with their ordinary happenings (things you are aware of) and even the ones you are not aware of (extraordinary happenings) are going on perpetually. At every moment tissues, cells and body and senses are passing through life and death. They are processed but due to in-adequate experience one cannot understand them. However, when a student of Yoga concentrates on the light of Purusha, he understands the drama of nature and the experience of life and death processes with their attending events. When the process of life and death are realized, one can over come all Karmas by the faster motion of Samyama. Many incarnations (past lives) can be passed by means of a dream experience. Therefore a student of Yoga is saved from going into another incarnation for that experience only. As long as Absolute Life (light of Purusha) is not realized, slow-and fast-moving Karmas cannot be experienced. The real practice of Samadhi begins at this point, where the student cannot do, think or wish anything that brings the sensation of physical, mental or spiritual death. The application through knowledge is to understand right as right and wrong as wrong. When this knowledge is obtained it manifests Eternal Existence, knowledge and Bliss.

### 24. Maitrdishu Balami

By performing Samyama on friendship, mercy etc. (Sutra 1.33) the student of Yoga excels in those respective human qualities (characteristics).

By performing Samyama over friendliness etc. are born the powers of friendliness etc.

Friendliness, compassion and mercy are three great feelings. By feeling friendliness and fellowship for living beings that are in happiness, one discovers the mental and moral power of friendliness and fellowship. By feeling compassion for those who are miserable and suffering, one discovers the power of compassion. By feeling joy for those who are disposed to merit, he discovers the power of joy. By developing neither hate or love for sinners, he cultivates the power of judgment and impartiality. As a result of cultivating these feeling and sentiments, powers of unfailing conscious energy of Samadhi (cosmic consciousness) arise.

25. Baleshu Hast-Baladeeni

Through performing Samyama on the strength of the elephant and others, power comes to the Yogi.

By performing Samyama on the power of an elephant one feels that strength of an elephant or anything with great strength. By performing Samayama on various powers, one obtains strength comparable to that of the strongest creatures on the planet.

For those that have not had the opportunity to ride an elephant I assure you the power beneath you is enormous. I cannot even think of any comparison that the average American could even begin to associate it with except by imagination. The message here is that infinite energy is at the disposal of anyone if he only has the power of wisdom and knows how to obtain it. In India, the elephant is the symbol of constructive force and a lion is the symbol of destructive force. So by discovering the powers of the mind, one will obtain all powers and forces.

Cryptechtesia, which includes clairvoyance, clairaudience and supernormal perception at a distance, telechesia, teleganosis, telekinesis etc. is now being discussed in the following Sutras.

The phrase "performing samyama" means to execute Dharana (concentration), meditation (dhyana), and contemplation (Samadhi) simultaneously (Sutra 3.3).Once you are able to perform samyama, then you might be able to attain the following powers. The following powers are those that are available to you.

26. Pravrityaloka-Nyasat Suhshma-Vyavahita-Viprakrista-Jmanam

With performing Samyama on the effulgent (bright light) (Sutra 1.36) comes the knowledge of the fine, the obstructed and the remote.

By directing the light of higher sense-activity toward those places or circumstances, the knowledge of the subtle, the veiled and the remote are obtained. By performing Samyama on the shining and radiating effulgent light (Sutra 1.30) he (the yogi) manifests intuitive knowledge of the subtle, the veiled and the remote.

When a Yogi performs Samyama—on the effulgent light in the heart, he sees things that are very remote. Things for instance, that happen at a distant place and are obstructed by mountain barriers and things which are very fine. The Inner Light, the effulgent light, has been explained as the light of Sattva (tranquil) substance, the principle of consciousness, which is clear, shining, radiating and all penetrating. When a Yogi perceives the light, he sees things that are veiled and concealed. He sees things, which are remote, things that are happening in a distant place. By performing Samyama on this light, inner consciousness is revealed. It is beyond time and space and is all-inclusive. Hence a student of Yoga obtains Cryptechtesia.

27. Bhuvanajnam Surye Samyama

By performing Samyama on the sun, comes the knowledge of the word.

From performing Samyama on the sun arises knowledge of the regions of the universe. The sun is said to be the soul of the manifested universe. Evolution, maintenance and involution of the universe depend upon the sun. The manifested universe is nothing but various forms of solar energy. The sun is the direct manifestation of the Supreme, while other manifested things of the universe are evolutes of the sun.

I should remind readers that the previous Sutra and the following Sutra were written at least 1500 years before the telescope was invented.

28. Chandra Taravyuha-Jnanam

By performing Samyama on the moon comes the knowledge of stars. By performing Samyama on the moon gives knowledge of the planetary system.

The moon is directly related to the sun. There are two paths of a Yogi: the first of which is the path of the sun, which means direct communication for the individual consciousness with the Supreme, in the same way as the sunlight is the direct manifestation of the Supreme. This state is obtained in Samprajnata Samadhi, cosmic consciousness. The second is the path of the moon, which means indirect communication of individual consciousness with the Supreme, in the same way as the moon-light is the indirect manifestation of the Supreme. Moonlight is nothing but reflected sunlight. The mind of a beginner is like the reflection of the moon. The meditation of a beginner is peaceful and successful when the moon is full. But when he is advanced his mind becomes directly related to the sun; and he attains a higher meditation without any interruption. Patanjali used these terms in the internal and external senses, physical and metaphysical relationship. In a physical sense, study of the star systems is possible only at night because the stars are obscured in daytime by the light of the sun.

29. Dhruve Tad-Gati-Jnamam

By performing Samyama on the polar star comes the knowledge of the motions of the stars. By performing Samyama on the polar star, one produces knowledge of the relative motions and positions of the stars.

30. Nabhi-Chadre Kaya-vyuha-jnam

By practicing Samyama on the circle of the navel, one gains the knowledge of the constitution of the body.

31. Kanta-Kupe Ksuth-Pipasa-Nivruttih

By performing Samyama on the pit of the throat, or stomach come cessation of thirst and hunger, in this way one can gain victory over them.

32. Kurama-Nadyam Sthairyam

By performing Samyama on the center of equilibrium and gravity, one can obtain steadiness of individual consciousness. This center is the nerve called Kurma.

In the state of Samadhi, when the nerve centers are well organized, psychological consciousness becomes free from organic operations and is firmly and steadily established in its omniscience, omnipotence and omnipresence. When human consciousness reaches beyond gravity centers, it begins to feel a mighty magnetic ocean flowing everywhere with lights and radiating energy of utmost self-confidence, self-satisfaction, self-realization and unity with Self and it does not want to leave that state. This is unique firmness which cannot be understood without experience.

33. Murday-Jyotishi Sidda-Darshanam

By performing Samyama on the light emanating from the top of the head will come sight of the Siddhas.

Through coronal light comes the vision of the perfected souls. By performing Samyama on the effulgent light of the Supreme in the center of the head, liberated and perfected souls have direct perception.

The halos around Mother Mary and other perfected souls are the same type of auras that Patanjali discusses in this Sutra. They can be seen by some and not by others, and it takes practice to be able to see them. When practicing Samyama on a Holy person make sure there is a white background and that your thoughts are clear when you start to practice Samyama on his coronal area.

### 34. Pratibhad Va Sarvam

With practicing Samyama on the effulgent light of the Purusha (true self which is God) comes all knowledge through the power of Pratibha.

All these can come without any Samyama to the person who has the power of Pratibha, spontaneous enlightenment from purity. When a person has risen to a high state of Pratibha, he has that great light. All things are apparent to him. Everything comes to him naturally without practicing Samyama. Pratibiha is intuitive knowledge, which is the forerunner of discriminative knowledge, in the same way that dawn is the forerunner of sunrise.

### 35. Hridaye Chitta-Samvit

By performing Samyama in the heart, there comes the knowledge of the Chitta. By concentrating psychic energy on the effulgent light in the heart, the individual mind obtains knowledge of Cosmic Mind.

### 36. Satva-Purushayor Atyantasamkeernayoh Pratyayavishesho

Enjoyment consists in the non-discrimination of the soul and Sattva (tranquil state) which are totally different, because the latter exists for a different state.

While performing Samyama on the centered self, one receives knowledge of the Purusha. Your experience results from the absence of the notion of distinction between the self and the objective essence of matter, which in fact are quite distinct from each other, because the latter exists for other reasons. Performing Samyama on that which exists for itself will give rise to the knowledge of the Purusha. Material enjoyment and relative experience consist of non-discrimination between psychic mechanism and psychic process: Psychic determination is non-self and it exists for the sake of Purusha, true Self, while the former is Self and self-existent. By performing Samyama on the principle of self-existence, self-knowledge is revealed.

All actions of Sattva (tranquility), a modification of Prakruti characterized by light and happiness, is for the Soul. When Sattva is free from egoism and illuminated with the pure intelligence of Purusha, it is called the self-centered one because in that state it becomes independent of all relations. For self-knowledge the analysis and knowledge of non-self is as important as the analysis and knowledge of Self. Self is distinct from the process of the psychic mechanism, Buddhi (intellect) which predominates in Sattva characteristics and which consists of sense organs, mind, ego-consciousness and non-differentiated Prakruti (nature).

Self is pure consciousness, pure existence, knowledge and bliss. Of all the evolutes of Prakruti, Sattva, Buddhi (intellect) the Self is of great importance. The senses present their objects to the mind, to ego-consciousness, this in turn to super consciousness or the tranquil intellect, which then in turn exhibits them to the Purusha (true self) in the realm of reality. It is Sattva (tranquility) intellectual (Buddhi) and psychic mechanism, which determines and discriminates the difference between Self and non-self as they work for Purusha and its enjoyment, experience and liberation from non-self. Buddhi (intellect) with its full staff; ego, mind, sense and body are engaged in its psychic processes, psychic determinism, with the help of consciousness which is inherent in Purusha, just as men work by the aid of light which is adjacent to it they become conscious of its form and then accomplish its experience of all objects.

Psychic processes that are a product of Prakruti are non-self and non-conscious in nature; still they appear to be Self and self-conscious. Buddhi (psychic principle), predominates in the Sattva quality of Prakruti, hence it is transparent in character. But Buddhi itself changes into its forms, much like an electronic force changes into various forms according to external objects as on television or in films. The light of Purusha is reflected on this modification of Buddhi and this modification of Buddhis is reflected in Purusha (Supreme Soul).

As a consequence of this mutual reflection, "I see," "I exist," "I am," I am happy," "I am sad," etc., certain experiences arise. For example, in the phrase, "I think," thinking is the process of psychic mechanism and "I" is a reflection of Purusha. It is extremely difficult to discriminate between the two. When someone says "I exist because my house exists," it is an indirect proof of self-existence. Neither the thinking mechanism nor the mechanism of the house is Self. It is difficult in relativity to present the Purusha, directly. The union of Budhhi produces a notion such as "I know", with the reflection of Purusha or true self.

The reflection of Purusha on psychic process, and the reflection of psychic process on the Purusha are simultaneous with the unity of the reflecting Purusha, and the particular modification of Buddhi (psychic process or intellect). The relationship between Self, Purusha, and Buddhi, and the psychic process associated with it is as such that the mental processes are interpreted as the experience of Purusha (true self,which is God).

Purusha, though entirely distinct, forms the nature of the psychic processes. Buddhi (intellect) has direct contact with Buddhi and indirectly is in touch with senses and the rest of the body. It is the witness of the states of psychic processes, (intellect or Buddhi), without intervention or intermediary. It is the Drasta, Seer, of senses, body and world by means of Buddhi without intervention or intermediary. The free and distinct Purusha becomes the witness when connected with Buddhi, psychic processes and psychic principle. Bondage is the reflection of the non-self into Self and liberation is the freedom from this reflection. When Buddhi (intellect) reflects self into self and non-self into non-self, suffering ends. When all suffering ends one attains enlightenment. Self, which is eternal existence, consciousness and bliss, is absolutely contrary to the "end of suffering" in quality. Relative experience fails to distinguish between the two. Self and non-self are not commingled, although even in relativity the dealing with the "end of suffering" is carried on without the discrimination of Self and non-self. Samadhi (absolute contemplation) is not in the realm of relativity. There is nothing that is really comparative to it. In short, in Samadhi, time, space, cause and effect have no room. By performing Samyama on Purusha (true self which is God), which is Self-shining, Self-radiating and Self-existent, one kindles the flame of knowledge of Purusha, which destroys ignorance completely. In doing so, one realizes Purusha as Pure-Existence, Consciousness and bliss. Only the light of Purusha, not by any other light, can know Purusha just as the light of itself can know the sun itself.

How is one to know that the knowledge obtained in Samadhi is by Purusha (the true self) or just simply the Prakruti (nature)? In performing Samyama on Purusha there will be progressive manifestations of extrasensory perceptions as milestones to show the manifestation of Brahman (the omnipresent, omnipotent and omniscient or God).

37. Tatah Pratibha-Sravana-Vedana-Adarsha-Asvada-Vartta Jayante

From those progressive manifestations of extrasensory perceptions arises the knowledge belonging to Pratibha (which is defined in the next paragraph), and supernatural hearing, touching, seeing and smelling. Intuition and the highest sensitivity of supernatural hearing, touching, seeing, tasting and smelling, however, precede this. Extrasensory perceptions and sensations of sound, touch, sight, taste and smell precede them.

While performing Samyama on Purusha (true self), the limitations of the senses are removed and their thresholds extended. Consequently there arises extrasensory perception through all sensory organs. There is a faculty of perception and sensation, which can perceive and sense without disturbing the present means of sensation and perception for sensory organs. This faculty is called Pratibha. The real sensory organs are very subtle and transcend the present sensory apparatus. When the real sensory organs are awakened by the practice of Samyama on Purusha, they can produce divine knowledge, hearing, touch, sight, taste and smell. By divine hearing come all the sounds of the universe. With divine vision comes the perception of heavenly colors. By divine taste comes the presence of divine tastes. By divine smell comes presence of higher odor. These extrasensory perceptions are signposts and milestones to indicate the progression of Samyama in the course of self-analysis. Hence, they should be used as means but not the ends. If they are used as means the meditator measures his/her progress in meditation by them and overcomes doubts and other obstacles. Otherwise these extrasensory perceptions may become stumbling blocks in the progress of self-realization.

38. Te Samadha Vupasarga Vyutthane Siddhaya

These are obstacles to Samadhi, but they are powers in the worldly state.

Although they are attainments to the outgoing Chitta (the fully restrained mind-composite), they are obstacles to the achievement of trance. These supernatural powers are obstacles to achieving Samadhi.

This is the most controversial of Patanjali's Sutras. It seems contradict the previous Sutras. If these supernatural powers are obstacles to Samadhi, why mention them? If you obtain these powers through Samadhi, why not use them? How is reading someone's mind going to get you to the ultimate goal of obtaining oneness with the ultimate Supreme Being? If you obtain these powers and tell no one about them, what good are they? They are to be used as milestones to your final progression. If you go around showing them off, charging people to read their minds, you will become forever attached to them. You might end up on David Letterman or Jay Leno but you will not achieve Samadhi. If you use them only as milestones, they will be a helpful way to allow you to measure your own progression to the ultimate goal. Only through your own Self-analysis will you know if you can obtain them and not become attached to them.

39. Bandha-Karana-Shaithilyat Prachara-samvedanat Cha Chittaasya Parshereera-Aveshah

When the cause of bondage of the Chitta has become loosened, the Yogi, by his knowledge of its channels of activity, the nerves, enters another's body. The Chitta may enter another body by relaxing the cause of its bondage and knowing of the routes through which it should pass.

As a result of slackening the causes of bondage and as a result of the free and penetrative flow of consciousness, mind-composite enters the body of others.

By virtue of the latent deposit of Karmas, the central organ mind-composite, which is changeable and unstable at every moment, becomes established in one body; and this is referred to as its bondage. Consequently, the penetrating power of mind-composite becomes free from Rajoguna and Tamoguna by the Karmas. As a result of the free flow of penetrative consciousness of mind-composite, a Yogi, by withdrawing mind-composite from his body, can penetrate others bodies. The senses accompany the mind-composite. Penetration is an inherent property of the mind. This is a tool that faith healers use. By this power anyone's mind can penetrate anyone else's. This power of penetration is greater or lesser according to the flow of mental consciousness. When a Yoga Teacher teaches, his mind projects into the minds of his students. Penetration is an eternal law of the mind. The causes of penetration are: slackening of Karmas, which are the causes of bondage; and attainment of knowledge of which is the cause of freedom. Penetration has two types of energy, attraction and repulsion. Attraction draws people toward one another and repulsion thrusts them anyway. Love is the cause of attraction and hate is the cause of repulsion. Accomplished Yoga teachers by this type of penetration, can teach their students, remove their grief and purify their minds.

40. Udanajayat Jala Panka Kantakadisu Asamga Utkrantishcha

By conquering the current called Udana, the Yogi does not sink in water or in swamps; he can walk on thorns and can die at will.

Mastery over Dyana, a category of bio-energy, results in ascension and non-contact with water, mud, thorns, etc. When one attains mastery over Udana by performing Samyama, one obtains the power of invulnerability to water, mud thorns, nails and in doing so the wins victory over death.

41. Samana-Jayat Javalanam

By the conquest of the current called Samana [a Yogi] is surrounded by a blaze of light.

Mastery over Samana, another category of bio-energy, contributes to radiant heat. This Samana also includes the heat-regulating center and the chemical center in the central nervous system. Temperature of the body can be increased or decreased by the control of Samyama. When a Yogi obtains victory over Samana, he may produce a blaze of light.

This is a special type of concentration in which the Yogi can produce a fire element from his body. Aura and astral bodies are projections of Samana. Every being is projecting light around itself but everyone does not see this light. By practice of higher meditation, one can see this light around every being.

This is one power I obtained 26 years ago before I started practicing Yoga on a regular basis. I was introduced to it at the Edgar Cayce Foundation in Virginia Beach, Virginia by Edgar Cayce's grandson. One of the techniques to see auras was introduced to me as a Cub Scout. Opposite colors of the American flag, red, white and blue, were in a magazine for Boy Scouts. The activity required you to focus, concentrate (dharana) on the opposite colors then quickly remove the picture from your sight and stare at a white surface. The red, white and blue flag seemed to briefly appear on the white surface . I can see auras around most people. A few of my students have said they have seen mine.

Years ago, pop legend Neil Diamond had a hit that included the lyric "turn on your love light let it shine for all the world to see." The light he mentions can be thought of as an Aura. When you turn on your love light, so to speak, those capable of seeing Auras will see yours.

42. Shratrakashayoh Sambandha-Samyamad Dvyam Shrotram

By performing Samyama on the relationship between the ear and Akasha one achieves divine hearing.

Akasha has been defined as the ether of space. Without space there can be no sound. By performing Samyama on the power of the higher sense of hearing and by listening to Nadam, Akasha, one obtains divine hearing.

Akasha, or hearing has been defined as Brahman, Saguna Brahman. This Saguna Brahman shines everywhere and radiates with all energy everywhere; therefore it is called Akasha in this context and is defined as complete shining (A=means completely, Kasha=means radiating or shining). As I pointed out in a previous Sutra on pranayama, Akasha has also been defined as "ether of space". Using the second definition Akasha is manifested in the Sahasrararm cerebrum, in the form of divine music. In the beginning it is manifested as a "ringing" sound and it gradually increases in volume and pitch and occupies various centers in the central nervous system. Ultimately it vibrates the entire ocean or ether with various pitch and musical notes. It is not perceived of the hearing apparatus but is perceived by the inner sense of hearing. It may sound without an instrument, hence it is called Anhata Nada. It is heard by the inner sense directly, so it is called Sruti Veda or knowledge. Pranavah (humming), Om, Sphotam, Anahata Nadam, sound current, Sabda and Akasha are synomyms in this instance. The practice of Nadam is the best way of leading one to Cosmic Consciousness. This sound current is heard within, and one should listen to it with a concentrated mind. Many varieties of sounds are heard such as buzzing, rainfall, chirping of birds, roaring of the ocean, stringed and percussion musical sounds. When Nadam is heard, one should know and understand that Kundalini (coiled power within) is awakening and that this sound is heard from Sushumna. A student of Yoga who desires to attain master of Yoga, should abandon all thoughts and with a carefully concentrated mind practice Shanmukhe, also known as Nada Yoga, Shabda Yoga or Sahaja. Evil tendencies, like serpents, renounce evil nature and begin to dance with the waves of sound. Self-effulgent consciousness is united with it. The mind loses all its wandering tendencies and all modifications; and becomes absorbed in Akasham, which is Brahman (Atman), free from all Upadhis (ignorance). The conception of Akasha as the generator of sound exists as long as sound is heard.

Bondless Akasham is called Parambabrahma, Paramatma, and Nirguna Brahma. By constant practice of concentration on Nadam through Shanmukhi (Yoga technique), all sins are destroyed. The mind and Prana become absorbed in Niranjana, Brahma-consciousness, and the student of Yoga reaches beyond the waking state, dream state, dreamless state, and trance state.

43. Kaya-Kashayoh Sambandha-samyanat Laghutulasamapatteshcha Akasha Gamanam

By performing Samyama on the relation between the Akasha and the body, you become as light as cotton.

Through meditation on them (the relation between the Akasha and the body), the Yogi goes through the skies. By performing Samyama between the relation of the body with ether of space, or by attenuating thought transformation to the lightness of cotton, movement through space becomes possible. By performing Samyama on the relationship between body and ether one attains lightness like cotton to the body and it attains levitation in space.

Space and time are omnipresent. Where is there a place where infinite space is not present? Even within the tiny atom space is present. If space within the earth were removed, it would be transformed into a small ball and even in this condition it would still contain space. The body is made of the same electromagnetic forces that govern planets and stars in space. Planets, with their mighty weight, are moving in space with incredible speed, because they are directly connected with these forces. So too do forces of gravity control the human body. When the body becomes directly related to magnetic forces by means of Samyama on relationship of body and space, it will obtain the speed and velocity of magnetic forces and will have the power of roaming through space at will. The psyche is beyond space, time, cause, effect and gravity. It is attached to the body by the forces of Rajas and Tamras. When by meditation, these forces are overcome the student feels the sensation of levitating in the air.

44. Bahir Akalpita Vrittir Mahavideha Tatah Prakasha Avarana Kshayah

Performing Samyama on the "real modifications" of the mind outside of the body is called the great-disembodied ness and with it comes the disappearance of the covering of light.

The actual passing out of the Chitta, and acting outside of the body is called the great Excorporeal or astral projection, which destroys the gloss of functional knowledge of the intellect. By performing Samyama on Mahavideha, the external modification of the mind-composite becomes real, and with that comes the destruction of the ignorance that conceals the nature of reality.

Everyone can potentially penetrate another person's body but this penetration is not actually physical. As I pointed out in the introduction to this chapter, sometimes a person can read another person's mind exactly and sometimes he cannot. So this penetration is of two kinds: Kalpita (imaginary) and Akalpita (actual). In an imaginary penetration, one reads another person's mind by their signs and moods, and this type of penetration is superficial. In actual penetration, the mind directly penetrates all states of mind-composite, whether conscious, unconscious, subconscious, subconscious or super-conscious.

The first penetration is Videhea, incorporeal, which means that it penetrates body and mind. The second penetration Mahavideha or supra incorporeal, which means that it penetrates all states of mind-composition. Mahvidaeha is an imminent and transcendent penetration of mind-composite. One does not need to read any signs and moods of body to read and or to penetrate the body and mind. Everyone has imaginary penetration into another's body but by practicing concentration one can achieve a higher penetration (Vidheha), and by advanced Samyama, one attains the highest and absolute penetration of body and mind-composite. By the power of Mahavideha, a liberated Yoga Teacher can enter the bodies of students and remove their afflictions, obstacles, tendencies, Karmas and ignorances, all of which conceals darkness conceal the nature of Ultimate Reality. Everyone inherently has the light of the Supreme but due to ignorance this Supreme light is concealed and unreality is projected, consequently one suffers. By performing Samyama on Mahavideha this darkness of ignorance is removed and destroyed and the eternal light of Sattva (serenity or tranquility) dawns, free from Rajas (darkness) and Tamas (Power and enjoyment).

The realm of Ego-consciousness is the middle state of knowledge. Mind consciousness is subjective consciousness in which one know no distinction of self and non-self just an infant has no subjective and objective distinction. The mind is the principle of pleasure. The whole subject and object are only for pleasure. This is the state of Tamas whose characteristics are power and enjoyment.

Ego-consciousness is the principle of reality, which distinguishes the self from the non-self and defines the real nature of the pleasure principle. This is the world of relativity. Ignorance is slackened here and the energy of Rajas (darkness) is manifested fully. Super-consciousness Buddhi (intellect) defines the nature of ultimate reality and plays the judicial role over ego-consciousness, which plays the role of the executive. In this state, consciousness reaches beyond subject and object relativity by means of the transcendental knowledge of Sattva (tranquility) and Purusha reflected in Sattva, the principle of consciousness. (Which can be very difficult to understand to for a casual observer who has never had any experience of meditation). However, when a Yogi reaches this state, all covering over of knowledge disappears and darkness and ignorance vanish. He becomes the soul of all souls and everything appears to him to be a manifestation of knowledge, of Purusha (true self which is God) and Brahman (Infinite Supreme Being).

45. Stula-Svarupa-Sukshama-Anvaya-Arthavatta-Samyamad Bhuta-Jayah

By performing Samyama on the different forms of elements and their essential traits and Gunas (qualities); and then to their contributions to the experience of the soul, comes mastery of the elements.

By performing Samyama on gross matter, its essential forms, its essential subtle components, its compounds, molecules, elements, atoms, tanmantras, ultra-atomic particles and their purposefulness, you will attain victory over matter and energy.

The Yogi can perform Samyama on the elements, first on the gross and then on the finer states. This Samyama is taken up more by a certain sect of the Buddhists. They perform Samyama on a lump of clay and gradually they begin to see the fine materials in it and obtain power over it. The same is done for potentially all the elements. The first word in the Sutra, Stula, means the physical form of the universe as it is perceived by the senses. Used in this context, the second word savarupa, means "essential forms of matter and nature," such as solid, liquid, gas, light and ethereal. The entire universe of matter and nature is divided into these five classes. Any object is exchangeable into any other of these forms by the addition or subtraction of energy, matter and nature. Matter and nature are one homogeneous ocean of energy, although they are present to the senses in their various essential forms. One thing is common among all: they are all matter and nature. Sukshama, the subtle, consists of the essential components of matter:

compounds, molecules, elements, atoms, and ultra-atomic particles, such as electrons, protons, and neutrons.

46. Tato Animada-Pradurbhavah Kaya-Sampad Tad Dharm AnaBhighatashca

From that come minuteness and the rest of the powers, glorification of the body, and indestructibility of the bodily qualities.

As a result there is the attenuation and other powers, which also leads the body to perfection by becoming immune to the elemental characteristics. From mastery over matter, energy and elements, one obtains manifestation of the supernatural powers of minuteness and the rest, as well the perfection of the body and mind, and the realization of the indestructibility of the qualities of matter, energy and elements.

This means the Yogis have attained the eight powers. He can make himself as minute as a particle or as huge as a mountain, as heavy as the earth or as light as the air; he can reach anything he likes, he can rule everything he wants, he can conquer everything he desires and so on. A tiger will sit at his feet like a lamb and all his desires will be fulfilled at will. Animadi consists of the following eight supernatural powers: (1) Anima, is power of being as minute as an atom. (2) Laghima, are lightness, buoyancy, and the power of being light. (3) Mahima, the power to expand oneself into space. (4) Gharima power to grow as heavy as anything (5) Prapte, is power to reach anywhere, even to other planets, fulfilling all wishes and desires. (6) Vashitvati, is the power of command over all. (7) Ishitvam, is power of evolution, maintenance and dissolution. (8) Yatra Kamavasayitva, is power to change destiny.

47. Rupa-Lavanya-Bala-Vajra-Samahananatvani Kayasampat

The glorification of the body is beauty, complexion, strength and adamantine (unyielding) hardness.

The perfection of the body consists in beauty, grace, strength or adamantine hardness. The body becomes indestructible; nothing can injure it. Nothing can destroy it until the Yogi wishes. An unknown author wrote, "Breaking the rod of time, he lives in this universe with his body." There is no more disease, death or pain, for him.

48. Grahan-Svarupa-Asmitanvayarthatvattva Samyamad Indriya-Jayah

By performing Samyama on the objectivity and power of illumination of the organs(the process of knowing) the substantive appearance, the egoism, the conjunction and the purposefulness of sensation one attains the mastery over the senses.

When perceiving an external object the organs leave their place in the mind and go towards the object. This process is followed by knowledge. Egoism is also present in the act. When the Yogi performs Samyama on these and the other two by gradation, he conquers the organs. Take up anything that you see or feel; a flower for instance. First, concentrate the mind on it, then on the knowledge that is in the form of a flower, and then on the ego that sees the flower and so on. By that practice all the organs will be conquered.

49. Tato Manuavitvam Vikarana-Bhavah Pradhana Jayahcha

From the process explained in the previous Sutra comes to the body the power of rapid movement like the mind power of the organs acting independently of the body and to the conquest of nature.

Then comes quickness of the mind and control of the senses. The self obtains the speed of mind, the power to perceive without sensory apparatus and one can conquer nature.

Just as by the conquest of the elements comes glorified body, so from the conquest of the organs will come the powers mentioned above.

50. Sattva-Purusanyata-Khati-Matrasya Sarva-Bhavadhisthatrutvam Sarva-jnatrutam Cha

With performing Samyama on the discrimination between Sattva and the Purusha comes omnipotence and omniscience. By performing Samyama on the Buddhi (intellect) one attains the psychic process of determinism, as well as Pure Self-knowledge.

One who is grounded in pure Sattva (tranquility) of Buddhi (intellect) and pure self-knowledge of their Purusha (true self) obtains supremacy over the entire manifested world of Prakruti (nature). Omnipotence and Omniscience is realized when a Yogi frees himself from all the other material attractions while resting in pure Sattva (tranquility) and Purusha and reflecting in this state. This Siddhi perfection, is called Vishoka, "meaning devoid of all sorrow". Reaching this state a Yogi becomes free from all sorrow, affliction and obstacles except in seed form.

51. Tad-Vairagyad Api Dosha-Beeja-Kshaye Kaivalyam

Giving up even these powers causes the destruction of the very seed of evil, which leads to Kaivalyam (independence from the material world).

From having no desires even for that (the supernatural powers), the seed of bondage, the conjunction to Purusha with Prakruti, having been destroyed, there arises Kaivalyam, consciousness absolute. Non-attachment to even these powers, omnipotence and omniscience leads to the destruction of all the seeds of Karmas and consequently Nirvanam is manifested.

Once again Patanjali appears to contradict himself. He states that even if you attain these eight powers you would have to give them up to attain absolute oneness with the Infinite Supreme Being—in essence Nirvana. Once again I will refer "to Christ's lesson it is easier for a camel to pass through the eye of a needle, than a rich man through the gates of heaven." These powers of the Yogi are attachments that prevent one from reaching Heaven, a state similar in many ways to Nirvana.

If a Yogi were to obtain and then give up these supernatural powers he would gradate to aloneness, independence and freedom. When one gives up even the ideas of omnipotence and omniscience, there comes the entire rejection of enjoyment, of temptations from celestial beings. When the Yogi sees all these wonderful powers and summarily rejects them, he reaches the goal. This is very similar to Christ's rejections of Satan's offer to use his powers to be king of the material world in the desert on his forty-day fast. All powers are simply manifestations and are no better than dreams. Was there really a Satan, or was Christ actually only struggling with his own mind? Even omnipotence is a dream. It depends on the state of the mind. As long as there is a mind it can be understood, as the goal is beyond even the mind.

52. Stahanyupanimantrane Sanga-Samyakaranam Punaranistata-Praasangat

The Yogi should not feel allured or flattered by the temptations of celestial beings, or have fear of evil again.

Even when the presiding powers invite, there should be no attachment or smile of satisfaction, since contact with the undesirable again is possible. There must be complete destruction of attachment to matter and material enjoyment, and lack of pride and conceit in perfection of the attainment of omnipotence and omniscience.

53. Kshna-Tat-Karmayoh Samyamad Vivekajam Jmamam

With performing Samyama on a particle of time and its precession and succession comes discrimination. By performing Samyama on the moments and their succession, there arises knowledge born of discrimination.

54. Jati-Lakshana-Deshair-Anyhatamavadchhedat Tulyahaoh Pratipattih

Even those things that cannot be differentiated by species, sign and place even they will be discriminated by the previously mentioned Samyama.

Therefore from the discriminative knowledge obtained by performing Samyama on the moment and the succeeding moment, one obtains discernment of two similar events and things whose distinction cannot be measured or recognized by class, sign and place.

55. Tarakam Sarva-Vishayam Sarvatha Vishayam Akramam Cheti Viekajam

The saving knowledge is that knowledge of discrimination that simultaneously covers all objects, in all their variations. Nirvanic and absolute discriminative knowledge is that which simultaneously covers the entire objective universe in all aspects.

56. Sattva-Purushayoh Shuddhi-Samye Kaivahlyam iti

By the similarity of purity between the Sattva (tranquility) and Purusha (true self which is God) one obtains Kaivalyam (Independence).

When the mechanism of psychic determinism, mind-composite, Buddhi, (intellect) all come together and are purified and refined to the level of Purusha—Kaivalyam is obtained. It is said to be an incontrovertible and immutable fact.

# Chapter 4

# KAIVALYA PADA—ON INDEPENDENCE

1. Jammausadhi Mantra Tapah Samadhi Jah Siddhaya

Janma=birth, aushaddhi=herb, mantram=tapah=pain bearing asceticism, samadhi=equanimity, jah=born, siddhaya=psychic powers

Siddhis are born of practices performed in previous births, or by herbs, mantra, mantra repetition, asceticism, or by samadhi.

Patanjali begins this chapter by reviewing the methods by which the Siddhis can be obtained by the Yoga practitioner. Some people attain the Siddhis without practicing anything in this life. They do not know what they did to have these kinds of powers. This could be proof that they had done something in a past life to merit such powers in this life. Patanjali also offers us some clues about the people who obtain some experience through the ingestion of LSD and marijuana. The so-called "grass" is an herb. Psychedelic mushrooms could be considered cousins of herbs as well. However, whatever the substances or their effects, they are only temporary and should not be repeated for any length of time because one would begin to rely on them.

He further states that Siddhis can be obtained through japa (mantra repetition), reflection of God, or by asceticism. Tapas was defined in the Sutra 2.1 as "accepting pain and suffering as a purifying process that boosts will power and control of the mind."

The third way of obtaining Siddhis is through Samadhi, the proper procedure of concentration, meditation and contemplation. Yes, you can obtain Siddhis through some mind-altering drug, but the effects are only temporary. So, Siddhis should be obtained through the regular process and practice of Yoga and not from the outside world through external stimuli.

2. Jatyantara Parinamah Prakriti Apurat

Jatyantara=one species to another, parinamah=transformation, Prakriti=Nature, apurat=by the inflow

The transformation of one species into another is brought about by the influx of Nature.

3. Nimittam Aprayojakam Prakartiman Varanabhedas Tu tata Ksetrikavat

Nimittam=incidental cause, Aprayojakam=effortless, Prakartiman=toward Natures's evolution, Varan=obstacles, bhedah=remove, Tu=but, Tatah=from that, Ksetrikavat will remove

Incidental events do not directly cause natural evolution, they just remove the obstacles, much like a farmer removes the obstacles in a water course to his field.

As I pointed out in the introduction, Patanjali gives the example of how a farmer has to remove obstacles from a water-course to his field. The mind also wants to run to its original source of tranquility but there are many impediments that block its flow.

Your practices and your teacher do the job of an agriculturist. We bring nothing new; we only remove the obstacles so that the flow of consciousness will be continuous.

4. Nimana Cittany ASmita Matrat

Nimana=created, chittani=mind-composite, asmita=egoity, matrat=alone

A Yogi's state of ego alone is the cause of (other artificially) created minds.

5. Pravritti Bhede Prayojakam Cittam Ekam Anekesam

Pravritti=functions, bhede=difference, prayojakam=director, chittam=composite, ekam=one, anekesham=one of the many

Although the functions in the created minds may differ, the original mind-composite of the Yogi is the director of them all.

6. Tatra Dhyanajam Anasayam

Tatra=of these, dyamanjam=born of meditation, anasayam=free from Karmic impressions

Of these (functions) they are free from Karmic impressions through meditation.

7. Karmasuklakrsman Yoginas Trividham Itaresam

Karma=action, asukla=neither white, akrishman=nor black, of three kinds, good, bad and mixed

Dr. Rao writes that black signifies darkness or something bad, and that white signifies means something pure and good. It has been said that a Yogi's actions are neither good nor bad because they are performed with such equanimity that you cannot put them in either category.

Generally, a normal person's actions are good, bad and mixed. An example of the latter is the following: if a Boy Scout helps an elderly person across the street only for a merit badge, it is good for the elderly person but the motive is bad. Yogis do things without any thought of the reason or reward. Thus, the actions and the reward is good karma without desiring or expecting a reward in advance.

8. Tatah tatvipaka anugunamanm evabbhivyakith vasanam

Tatah=of these, tat=their, vipaka=fruition, anugunamam=favorable conditions, Eva=alone, Abhivyakith=manifestation, vasanam=subconscious impressions

Of these [actions] only those vasanas (subconscious impressions) for which there are favorable conditions of producing their fruits will manifest in a particular birth.

9. Jati Desakala Vyavahitaman Apy anantraryam apysamriti Saskarayoh Ekarupatvat.

Jati=class or species, desa=space, kala=time, vyavahitaman separated, apy=though, anantaryam=uninterrupted relationship, apysmriti=memory, saskarayoh=impressions, ekarupatvat=because identical

Although desires are separated from their fulfillments by class, space and time, they have an uninterrupted relationship because the impressions of desires and their memories are identical.

10. Tamas Manuavitvam Cases Nityatvat

Tasam=they (the impressions) anaditvam=have no beginning, cha= and, asishah=desire to live, nityatvat=eternal

Since the desire to live is eternal, impressions have no beginning.

11. Hetu Phalasrayalambanih Samgrhitatvad esam Abhave Tadabhavah

Hetu=cause, phala=effect, asraya=basis, alambanaih=support, samgrhitatvat=being held together, esham=these, abhave=with the disappearance, tat=they, abhavah=disappear

The impressions, being held together by cause, effect, basis and support, disappear with the disappearance of these four.

12. Atitanagatam Savarupato'sty Adhva Bhedad Darmanam

Atita=past, anagatam=future, Svarupatah,=own form, asty=exist, adhava=in the conditions, Bhedat=difference, dharmanam= characteristics

13. Te Vyakta Suksmah Gunamanah

Te=they (the characteristics), vyakta=manifest, sukshmah=subtle, gunatmanah=nature of the gunas

Whether manifested or subtle, these characteristics belong to the nature of the gunas (constituents of nature).

14. Parinaama Edkatvat vastu tattvam.

Parinama=transformations, ekatvat=due to the uniformity, vastu=things, tattvam=reality

The transformations of things or qualities are due to the uniformity of reality.

15. Vastu Samye Chitta bhedat tayoh Vibhaktah Pathah.

Vastu=objects, samye=same, chitta=minds, bhedat=due to differences, tayoh=their, vibhaktah=are different, panthah=ways of perception

Due to the differences between various minds, perceptions of even the same object may vary.

16. Na Caika Citta Tantram Vastu Tadapramanamkam Tada Kim Syat

Na=Nor, cha=and, eka=single, chitta=mind, tantram=dependent, vastu=object, tat=that, apramanakam=or perceived, tada=then, kim=what, wyat=becomes

Nor does an object's existence depend on a single object, known or unknown.

17. Tauparagapeksitvac Cittasya Vastu jnatjnatam

Tat=thus, uparaga=coloring apekshitvat=due to the need, chittasya=of the mind-composite, vastu=object, jnata=known, ajmatam=unknown

An object is known or unknown depending on whether or not the mind is colored by it.

18. Sada Jnatas Citta Vrttayas Tat Pra-Bhoh Pursaasyaparinamitvat

Sada=always, jnatah=know, chitta=mind-composite, vrittyah=modifitions, tat=its prabhoh=Lord, Purshasya=of the Purusha, aprinvamitvat=due to his changeless

Due to His changelessness, change in the mind-composite is always known to the Purusha, who is its Lord.

Here, Patanjali elucidates again the changes in the mind-composite. The chittam changes constantly because change is it's natural tendency. The Mind is a part of our ever-changing nature. However clever we are, we can only keep the mind quiet for a little while. Therefore, our aim is not to keep the mind peaceful, but to rise above the mind and realize the ever-peaceful Self. Purusha (true self which is God) is the owner of the mind-composite or as Patanjali puts it, its Lord. He knows all the changes that happen in it. How could He know them if He is also changing? A changing thing cannot recognize the changes in something else, like and insane person cannot recognize the insanity of another person if they both have similar types of insanity. Some examples would be drug addicts, alcoholics or religious fanatics. So Purusha, being changeless, can always recognize the changing nature of the mind.

19. Na Tat Svabhasam Drsyatavat

Na=not, tat=it (the mind-composite) svabhasam=self-luminous, drisyatvat=because of its perceptibility

The mind-composite is not self-luminous because it is an object of perception by the Purusha.

Here we see more or less the same idea conveyed in the previous Sutra. The mind-composite is not the subject; it is the object to the one subject, which is the Purusha. The mental functions are what you, as Purusha, perceive it to be. It would be difficult for the perceived to become the perceiver and vice-versa. Generally when a perceiver is perceived then he is no longer a perceiver but, rather, the perceived. To really possess this awareness, this isolation of perceiver and perceived, is Yoga.

It seems easy. However, Dr. Rao asked this question:—So why don't we always have it? Because the quality of the mind is not that clear. It still drags us down. It does not allow us to stay separated from the mind. Maya (illusion) tricks us."

He continues by stating, "You know that yesterday you had an experience on the mental level and it didn't bring you lasting satisfaction. 'You may say, I don't like it anymore and I don't want it.' This is the last time I will run after that." Then, two days later you want the same experience again. What does it mean? At a certain point, the true wisdom comes up, but then again maya (illusion) tricks you. 'Oh, yesterday it brought pain, but today it's going to be wonderful. Come on.'

That is because there is still ego, which is the basis of the mind. It does not allow you to know and be who you are. That is why, even though you are the Purusha, you do not always experience that. When you hurt because somebody hurts you, you should feel the same way, saying to yourself "Well, you did not hurt me, your mind did it, so I can not be angry with you."

When we hurt someone we put the blame on our mind. When somebody else does it, we usually say, "How dare you do that?" In savasana (the Hatha corpse pose) you may say, "I'm not the body; the body is just lying here." But when you get up, if somebody says, "Oh what a plump person you are", you become disturbed. The person didn't call *you* chubby. They called your *body* chubby.

This realization does not stay with us for long. However, we should try to retain that awareness always. It will slip away but you must bring it back again and again and again. That is the essence of spiritual practice.

20. Eka Samye Cobhayanavadharanam

Eka=one and the same, Samye=time, cha=and, uhhaye=both, anavadharam=cannot perceive

The mind-composite cannot perceive both subject and object simultaneously (which proves it is not self-luminous).

The mind-composite perceives objects outside. At other times, if it is clean enough, it can also turn inward and reflect the Purusha. So, it can be either subject or object. As a subject, it sees other things. As an object, it is seen by the Purusha. But the Purusha (true self) can never be both. It is always the subject.

21. Chittantara Drsye Buddhibuddheh Atiprasangah Smrtisamkaras Ca

Chittantara=another mind, drisyse=perception, buddhibuddheh=perceiver of perceivers, atiprasaangah=endlessness, smritisamkarah=confusion of memory, cha=and

If the perception of one mind by another mind is self evident, we would have to assume an endless number of them, and the result would be confusion of memory.

22. CiterApratisamkramamyasTadakara Pattaau Savabuddhisamvedanam

Chiteh=consciousness, apratisamkramayah=of Purusha is unchangeable, tat=it (chitta), akarpattau=by getting the reflection of the Purusha, svabuddhiamvedamam=becomes self-conscious

Consciousness of the Purusha (true self) is unchangeable, and the mind-composite becomes self-conscious through its reflection.

23. Drashttri Drsyoparaktam Cittaam Sarvartham

Drashttri=the Seer, drisya=the seen, uparaktam=being colored (affected) chittam=mind-composite, sarvartham=understand all.

The mind-composite when colored by both the Seer and seen, understands everything.

24. Tad Samkhyeha Vasanabhis Cittam Api Pararthatm Samhatya Daritvat.

Tat=that, asamkhyeya=countless, vasanbhih=through desires, chittam=mind-composite, api=also, parartham=for the sake of another, samhatya=in association (with the Purusha) karitvat=acting

Although having countless desires, the mind-composite exists for the sake of another (the Purusha) because it can act only in association with it.

25. Visea Darsina Atmabhava Bhavana Vinivrittih.

Vishesha=distinct, darsina=seer, Atambhava=mind as Self, bhavana=thoughts of mind and the Atman, Vinivrittih=thoughts of mind as the Atman cease forever

The distinction of the seer and the mind as Self through thoughts of mind and Atman (Supreme Soul), thoughts of Mind as the Atman cease forever.

26. Tadhai Viveka Nimnam Kaivalya Pragbharam Cittam.

Tadahi=then, viveka=discrimination, nimnam=inclines toward, Kaivalya=absoluteness, independence, Pragbharam=gravitating toward, Cittam=mind-composite

Then the mind-composite is inclined toward discrimination and gravitates toward Absoluteness.

27. Tacchidresu Pratyayantarani Sam-Skarebhyah

Tacchidreshu=in between, pratayayatarani=arise distracting thought, samskarebhyah=from past impressions

In between, distracting thoughts may arise due to past impressions.

28. Hanam Esam Klesavad Uktam

Hanam=removal, esham=their [old impressions] klesavad=as in the case of obstacles, uktam=has been said before

29. Prasmakhyane py Akusidasaya Sarvatha Vivkakhyater Dharmamegah Samadhih

Prasamkhyane=in the attainment of highest reward, due to perfect discrimination, apy=even, akusidasya=totally disinterested, sarvathta=constant, vivekakhyateh=discriminative discernment, dharmanmeghah=cloud of dharma, samadhi=contemplation

He who, due to his perfect discrimination, is totally disinterested in even the highest rewards retains constant discriminative discernment, which is called dharmamegha (cloud of dharma) samadhi. (Note: the meaning of dharma includes virtue, law, justice, law, duty, morality, religion, religious merit, and steadfast decree.)

Here, Patanjali talks about a samadhi called dharmamegah samadhi, the cloud of dharma. Dharmamegha means that all the beautiful characteristics are there. One attains that state when even the desire to be high is gone. Why? Because, who desires to get high? Certainly not the person who is already high. As long as one has the desire to get high, then he is not high. When you get high on music, drugs, church, the desire fades. When you attain what there is to attain all desires will fade. It is only then that you will be liberated.

I refer back to Jesus' statement, "It would be easier for a camel to pass through the eye of needle than for a rich man to pass through the gates of heaven." A beggar could be just as attached to his alms bowl as a rich man is to his yacht or mansion. It all comes down to attachments—material attachments, mental attachments, and even desires.

Saint Thirmoolar said, "Even with God, please be without desire." This suggests that the desire to be with God is also bondage. Ultimately, even the desire to be saved must be abandoned. Only then will you be unattached and "get God." Dr. Rao says that becoming without desire and the fulfillment of desire happen simultaneously. It is something like wishing for sleep until you fall asleep; and the desire is fulfilled, but you are not aware of its fulfillment.

So, you really cannot attain this darmamegah samadhi by wanting it. The effort of the desire keeps you from attaining it. Once the effort is gone it becomes effortless. In the meantime it is better to have good desires in order to stay away from the undesirable ones. Once you get rid of the bad ones, the good ones are easy to attain.

30. Tatah Klesa Karma Nirttih

Tatah=from the (samadhi) klesa=affliction, karma=action, nivrittih=cessation

From that samadhi all afflictions and karmas cease.

Dr. Rao writes, [By dharmamegha samadhi all that affects the mind goes away. One becomes a Jivanmukta. Such a person is not affected by anything. He is there and things happen; that person is a constant witness. The body and mind, which were trained well before liberation, just continue certain functions because of the prarabda, or residual Karma.]

To review the workings of Karma, all our actions are grouped into three sections. As previously stated, all karmas that are performed leave their results. Those results are stored in an imaginary bag called the karmashaya, which has been defined as, "the bag of karma".

Prarabda Karma is the portion taken out of the bag to be experienced in this life. According to Yoga science you have lived before in a number of different bodies and have performed many different actions. The results are now bundled up in the karmashaya. Sanjita karma is the total of all your past karmas. Prarabkda is the amount allotted for you to experience in this lifetime. It is according to your prarabda that you come into this world with different characteristics of body and mind. We are made male and female because in this life we each have to undergo certain experiences for which a certain type of body is needed.

While experiencing the prarabda we are creating new karmas. How can we distinguish between the prarabda and the agami, or new karma? Anything unforeseen that happens unexpectedly is due to prarabda. But anything that you consciously plan and then execute is your new karma. If you purposely kick a stone and hurt your foot, that is agami karma. If while just walking around, you suddenly hit your toe that is parabda. So these are the three kinds of karmas: sanjita, prarabda and agami.

In the case of Jivamuktas (realized saints), they have come into the world with human bodies because of their prarabda. Until they became liberated, they were just like anybody else, but with their self-knowledge they decided not to use any new karma to bind themselves, so there is no agami for them. But that does not mean they are not producing any actions. Some things do seem to be happening. They seem to be doing many things. But they are not. And because of this isolation from the mind and body, they are not affected by the reactions of the acts you see.

31. Tada Sarvavarana Malapedtasya Jmasyanatyaj Jneyam Alpam

Tada=then, sarva=all, avarana=coverings, malapetasya=removal of impuritites, jmamasya=of knowledge, anantyat=because of the infinity, jneyam=to be known, alpam=very little

Then all the coverings and impurities of knowledge are totally removed. Because of the infinity of the knowledge, what remains to be known is almost nothing.

What is impurity? Dr. Rao likens it to the sensitive coating on photographic film. The "I" and "mine" coat our mental film and then we want to catch everything they see. If it were not for the sensitive film, you may see many things, but they would not affect you, because nothing would get recorded. The mind of a Jivanmukta is like uncoated, crystal-clear mica sheet. It runs through the camera and pictures are shot, but nothing gets recorded. There is nothing to process, nothing to develop and nothing to fix. Which means the Jivanmuktas have no fixations.

32. Tatah Krtarthanam Parinama Krama Samptir Gunanam

Tatah=then, kritarthanam=having fulfilled their purpose, parinama=transformations, krama=sequence, samaptih=terminate, gunamam=gunas

Then the gunas terminate their sequence of transformations because they have fulfilled their purpose.

This is a beautiful Sutra to understand. Dr. Rao says the three gunas (sattva, rajas and tamas) constantly intermingle, and Prakriti (nature) functions thusly. Why should they do this? Why does nature function? Nature functions to give experience to the reflected Purusha, or the mind. The scriptures sometimes mention Purusha in this context, but what is meant is how the Purusha is reflected upon the mind-composite. Unfortunately, the Prakriti, of which our mental mirror is made, is itself made up of the three gunas, so it is not always the same. It is sort of a psychedelic mirror. Occasionally it is straight, but most of the time it moves around.

You forget the truth because you see it so rarely, whereas ugliness is nearly constant. You misconceive yourself as the changing images and lament, "Oh, I am terribly ugly, I am terribly unhappy." You put yourself in the position of the image. So, the duty of Prakriti is to torture the soul in every way until it gets enough knocks and bumps and you finally say, "I can not take it anymore."

Then at some point the soul in effect says, "No, I cannot be affected by all this I should stay away." When this understanding comes, the soul renounces the world. It says "I don't want you anymore, because the very moment I experience you, you always put me into difficult situations. You never allow me to be quiet. Now and then you give me a little happiness, but you seem to bring me mostly unhappiness." That is what is called sanyasa, or renunciation.

When you have had enough pain, the soul will detach itself and will no longer contain any impurities.

And then what happens to Prakritti or Nature? Dr. Rao offers the analogy of a mother with a number of children, who all go out to play and get dirty. When they return, totally covered with grime, she puts them into the bathroom and turns on the shower. Of course, she cannot clean everybody at the same time, so she washes them one by one. Once the baby is clean, what will she do with it? She takes it out of the tub and says, 'Go, get dry and hop into bed.' Will she stop working? No. There are still more dirty children in the tub. Mother Prakriti or Mother Nature is just like that. She does not stop functioning after cleaning just one child. She says, 'Okay you are clean. Go and don't come to me again. My job is over with you. But I still have a lot of work to do with other children.'

That is what is meant in this Sutra. Prakriti, the qualities and their continuous transformations, stop acting on a freed soul because they have fulfilled their purpose. They have given enough experience to the Purusha (true self) for its independence or liberation.

### 33. Ksana Pratiyogi Parinamaparanta Nirahyah Kramah

Kshana=moments, pratiyogi=uninterrupted succession, parinama=transformation, aparanta=end, nirgrah=grasped (recognized) kramah=sequence

The sequence referred to above means an uninterrupted succession of moments, which can be recognized at the end of their transformations.

### 34. Purusarthasunyanam Gunam Pratiprasavah Kaivlyam Svarupa Pratishta Kaivalyam Svarupa Pratishta Va Citisakter Iti

Purusharthasunyam=having no more purpose, gunanam=of the gunas, pratiprasavah=absorb, kaivalyam=absoluteness or independence, svarupa=its own nature, pratishta=settles in, va=or, chitisakteh=power of pure consciousness, iti=thus

Thus, the supreme state of Independence manifests while the gunas reabsorb themselves into Prakriti, having no more purpose to serve the Purusha. The power of pure consciousness settles in its own pure nature.

Patanjali does not mean that the gunas (constituents of Nature) and the Prakriti (Nature) are not the same. Prakriti is used when the gunas do not manifest separately. When the gunas manifest, Prakriti functions with the Purusha. Once the job is complete, the gunas withdraw and the power of Pure Consciousness settles in its own pure nature. It no longer needs outside stimuli for happiness because it is happiness personified.

# FINAL COMMENTARY

Before receiving my Degree of Master of Yoga Education, I was instructed to make my own commentary and examine the psychological events with my own human experience. It is for that reason that I want to include the results of my self-examination. I will point out again that it is not my intention to tell you what is truth and is not. I, like you, am still on the path and will arrive there eventually. Your experiences on the way will be similar and also dissimilar to mine. Check your experiences with *your* holy scriptures through; concentration, meditation and contemplation and then make your own self-examination by calming your mind and letting your individual suggestions be replaced by suggestions from a purer source. Knowing the difference between the two is Yoga.

In Sutra 1.7 on right knowledge, Patanjali specifically points out that scriptural testimony is right knowledge.

In Sutra 1.2. Patanjali says, Yoga Chitta Vritti Nirodah=Restraining the modifications of the mind-composite.

In Sutra 1.3 Patanjali says, Tada Dradhtuh svarupe vashanam=Then the seer rests in its own nature or state.

All four chapters of Patanjali's discourse are devoted to explaining how to accomplish Sutras 1.2 and 1.3. After everything you do, all your practice, meditations and good works, it will all come down to the true you resting in your natural blissful state.

You can still live and work in the world but nothing will affect your calm state. Think good thoughts and you will be good. Think great thoughts and you will become great. But think these thoughts for the benefit of others, not for your false ego or base self.

*Only a life lived for others is a life worthwhile.*
—Albert Einstein.

*Life's most urgent question is, what are you doing for others?*
—Martin Luther King Jr.

The practical truth is to live a dedicated life. That itself is "A path to Super-Conscious Bliss." Buddha said, "Before enlightenment I carried water and chopped wood. After enlightenment, I carried water and chopped wood."

In the book *"Jesus & Buddha—The Parallel Sayings"* the Editor published all the similar teachings of these two great men. The topics included their teachings and thoughts on everything from "Compassion" and "Wisdom" to "Temptation" and "Salvation". However, the Chapter that stood out in my mind after beginning this book was on the similarity of the "Miracles" both Buddha and Christ had performed in public.

In Jack Kornfield's Introduction to the book he pointed out that there has been for years popular speculation of Jesus having traveled to India during the "missing years" and was introduced to Budhhist teachings. Why is there no Scriptural Testimony of Jesus' whereabouts between the age of 13 and approximately 30 when he emerged to start his short but influential ministry that changed the course of History?

I have to agree with Mr. Kornfield that any explanation is unnecessary. The similarities are not the kind that suggest cultural borrowing. They are structural. Both these men simply had similar religious experiences.

Many people believe that Patanjali lived about two hundred years before Christ. Others believe that they could have been contemporaries. Regardless, just after Patanjali wrote the "Yoga Sutras," Christ performed in public almost all of the supernatural powers outlined in the second half of Chapter III of this book.

Proof that Christ performed these supernatural powers, which are called miracles, is found in the New Testament of the Bible and as Patanjali said, scriptural testimony is right knowledge.

Many theologians have written that Judas Iscariot was a member of a group called the Zealots. Barabas, who was freed in lieu of Jesus, was also a member of this violent group. It has been suggested that Judas became very upset when he learned that Jesus was not going to use his supernatural powers to wipe out the Romans and liberate Judea. However, Jesus explained to him in no uncertain terms that he was not going to kill anyone and that Judas should "love thine enemy." Judas betrayed Jesus; just as Christ had predicted, and he (Christ) was summarily executed.

Here are a few comparisons that might provide food for thought and contemplation. They have for me. However they are not proof of anything.

Sutra 3.41—By the conquest of the current Samana, he (the yogi) is surrounded by a blaze of light.

Mathew 6.22—The lamp of the body is the eye. If your eye is sound, your body will be filled with light.

Mathew 17.22—And he was transfigured before them; his face shone like the sun and his clothes became white.

(Note: Christ specifically told the witnesses not to tell anyone what they saw after the transfiguration until after his death.)

Sutra 3.16—By Performing Samyama over these three-fold changes, the knowledge of past and the future is obtained.

Mathew 17.22—As they were gathering in Galilee, Jesus said to the people, "The son of Man is to be handed over to men, and they will kill me, and he will be raised on the third day."

Sutra 3.40—By Conquering the current called Udana the Yogi does not sink in water or in swamps.

John 13. 37–38—The sea was stirred up because a strong wind was blowing. When they had rowed about three or four miles, they saw Jesus walking on the sea, and coming near the boat, and they began to be afraid. But he said to them "It is I, do not be afraid."

Sutra 3.42—By performing Samyama on the relationship between body and ether come lightness like cotton to the body and it attains levitation in space.

Sutra 3.19—By performing Samyama on the signs in another's body, knowledge of his mind comes.

John 13 37–38—Peter said to Jesus, "Master, why can't I follow you now? I will lay down my life for you." Jesus answered, "Will you lay down your life for me? Amen, Amen, I say to you, the cock will not crow before you deny me three times."

John 13–17—"Amen, amen, I say to you, one of you will betray me."(Speaking about Judas)

Sutra 3.21—By performing Samyama on the form of the body, the perceptibility of the form being obstructed, and power of manifestation in the eye being separated, the Yogi's body becomes unseen.

John 20.6—When Simon Peter arrived after him, he went into the tomb and saw burial cloths but rolled up in a separate place. Then the other disciple also went in, the one who had arrived at the tomb first, and he saw and believed.

Live a good life. To paraphrase what Buddha said, you can find bliss working in a garden, cooking food or chopping wood. You do not have to walk on water or float in the air, but those attainments are available to you. What one man can achieve so can another. But your desire to achieve those supernatural powers could be a hindrance to the ultimate goal—Oneness with the Infinite Supreme Being. Before walking on water we may want to learn how to jump over the gutter without killing ourselves.

So why not start by calming our minds so that we can make this world heaven through some of the techniques offered by our saints and sages. When we restrain the modifications that disrupt our minds, this is Yoga.

*If you want to change the world, start with yourself.*

—Mahatma Ghandi

Peace be with you, Shalom, and, as always, may the Divine Light in me greet and honor the Divine Light in you. Om Shanti, Shanti, Shanti.

# AUTHOR BIOGRAPHY

Sri Joseph Ketron has been practicing Yoga for 26 years. In recent years, he slowly intensified his devotion to Yoga. He received his Masters Degree of Yoga Education from High-Tech Yoga in Lowell, Massachusetts.

He is a member of St. Olaf's Roman Catholic Church in Williamsburg, Virginia, where he plays the drums and other percussion instruments at two masses a week. He currently teaches Flow Hatha Yoga for the Colonial Williamsburg Foundation at the Williamsburg Lodge and Sacred Grounds in Williamsburg. He also teaches Raja Yoga to select students.

The profits generated by the purchase of this book will go to help the World Peace Fund provide wells for Third World Nations. If you would like to make an additional contribution, please email Ketron0515@aol.com or write to:

Sri Joseph Ketron<br>
128 Davis Drive<br>
Williamsburg, Virginia 23185

0-595-25854-9

Sri Joseph Ketron has been practicing Yoga for 26 years. In recent years, he slowly intensified his devotion to Yoga. He received his Masters Degree of Yoga Education from High-Tech Yoga in Lowell, Massachusetts.

He is a member of St. Olaf's Roman Catholic Church in Williamsburg, Virginia, where he plays the drums and other percussion instruments at two masses a week. He currently teaches Flow Hatha Yoga for the Colonial Williamsburg Foundation at the Williamsburg Lodge and Sacred Grounds in Williamsburg. He also teaches Raja Yoga to select students.

The profits generated by the purchase of this book will go to help the World Peace Fund provide wells for Third World Nations. If you would like to make an additional contribution, please email <u>Ketron0515@aol.com</u> or write to:

Sri Joseph Ketron
128 Davis Drive
Williamsburg, Virginia 23185

$13.95 U.S.
$22.95 Canada
£11.99 U.K.

www.iuniverse.com